CU00607221

CityPack
Hong Kong

**SEAN SHEEHAN
AND PAT LEVY**

*Sean Sheehan and Pat Levy
lived in South-East Asia for
eight years, the last two of
which were spent in Hong
Kong. They have travelled
extensively in China, and first
visited the country in 1986 by
taking a slow boat from Hong
Kong to Shanghai along with
their two children, then aged
four and six. Sean Sheehan is
also the author of* CityPack
Beijing. *When they are not
travelling or writing, they
spend their time in West Cork,
Ireland, where their hobbies
are gardening and walking.*

For city-centre map see
inside back cover

AA Publishing

Contents

About this book...4

About this book

KEY TO SYMBOLS

✚ map reference on the fold-out map accompanying this book (see **MAPS** in main text below)

🚍 nearest bus/trolley/tram route

🛥 nearest ferry stop

✉ address

♿ facilities for visitors with disabilities

☎ telephone number

✋ admission charge

🕐 opening times

↔ other nearby places of interest

🍴 restaurant or café on premises or near by

❓ tours, lectures or special events

🚇 nearest Mass Transit Railway (MTR) station

➤ cross-reference (see below)

🚃 nearest overground train station

ℹ tourist infomation

ORGANISATION

CityPack Hong Kong's six sections cover the six most important aspects of your visit to Hong Kong.

- Hong Kong life – the city and its people
- Itineraries, walks and excursions – how to organise your time
- The top 25 sights to visit – from west to east across the city
- Features about different aspects of the city that make it special
- Detailed listings of restaurants, hotels, shops and nightlife
- Practical information

In addition, text boxes provide fascinating extra facts and snippets, highlights of places to visit and invaluable practical advice.

CROSS-REFERENCES

To help you make the most of your visit, cross-references, indicated by ➤ , show you where to find additional information about a place or subject.

MAPS

- **The fold-out map** in the wallet at the back of the book is a comprehensive street plan of Hong Kong. All the map references given in the book refer to this map. For example, the University Museum at 94 Bonham Road has the following information: ✚ B8 indicating the grid square of the map in which the museum will be found.
- **The city-centre maps** found on the inside front and back covers of the book itself are for quick reference. They show the Top 25 Sights, described on pages 24–48, which are clearly plotted by number (**1** – **25** , not page number) from west to east across the city.

PRICES

Where appropriate, an indication of the cost of an establishment is given by **£** signs: **£££** denotes higher prices, **££** denotes average prices, while **£** denotes lower charges.

HONG KONG *life*

INTRODUCING HONG KONG

Post '97

On the surface, little has changed in Hong Kong since the territory reverted to Chinese rule. 'Two systems, one nation,' has become a reassuring mantra for those who feared the collapse of Hong Kong's prosperity, and Hong Kong is now a model to which the rest of China aspires. Below the surface, however, the people of Hong Kong have enough political savvy to know that the years ahead are still uncertain.

A new era Hong Kong, so long a vestigial colony of the bygone British Empire, reverted to Chinese rule at midnight on 30 June 1997. The pragmatic citizens of Hong Kong took the transition in their stride and life now carries on as normal while people wait to see what history will bring. This is an unfolding drama in which you as a visitor to Hong Kong can share.

Island life Hong Kong Island is visually stunning. The Central area is filled with an astonishing array of skyscrapers that peer down on a contradictory mix of the materialistic and the spiritual. Everywhere people are frantically trying to make money, while under a flyover an old woman crouches to beat with a shoe a piece of paper that carries the names of her gossipy neighbours whose malicious influence will, she hopes, be crushed by this ancient magic ritual of *da siu yan* ('beating small people').

Sharing the incredibly congested space with the financial institutions and shopping centres are public housing blocks, where the lives of ordinary citizens have little in common with the surrounding glitz and glamour. Real estate costs in Hong Kong are expressed by the number of

thousand dollars to each square foot. Victoria Peak, a wooded 552m-high hill that looks down on Central and Victoria Harbour from the centre of the island, is home to the wealthiest tycoons and commands the very highest rents.

North to the border Hong Kong Island is only one part of Hong Kong, and just over five minutes by ferry across the harbour is the tip of the Kowloon Peninsula, called Tsim Sha Tsui. Here ritzy and not-so-ritzy shops and restaurants are packed together with a staggering density. North of this is the residential and shopping area of Mong Kok, which has the highest density of population on Earth. Here you will literally rub shoulders with residents and share the frustrations and frissons of a truly frenetic shopping experience.

Further north still are the New Territories, which stretch up to what is still the border with China. Now in the post-97 era most Hong Kong people are tied to their forebears across the border more closely than ever, and it is this cultural continuity that gives Hong Kong its unique appeal and fascination. This is no mere Chinatown; it is a Chinese city with pockets of Westernism where you are able to enjoy the best of both worlds.

Live to work

The work ethic is not an ideal in Hong Kong, it is simply a necessity of life. There are virtually no natural resources, only some 1,000sq km of land, and no unemployment pay or minimum wages.

The Star Ferry crosses the harbour, linking Kowloon and Hong Kong Island

A DAY IN THE LIFE OF A HONG KONGER

Gweilos

The literal translation for *gweilo* is 'ghost man' (*gweipor* means 'ghost woman'), originally coined as a derogatory label for the pale-faced colonial masters. Nowadays the term is generally used, often humorously, for Western expatriates (and tourists) whose presence in areas such as Wan Chai, especially at night, seems disproportionate given that they constitute less than 2 per cent of the

The day begins early, in the cool hours of the morning. Buying breakfast at a bakery, going to the park to practise *t'ai chi ch'uan* – the slow balletic exercise that gets the life energy moving smoothly around the body – or joining the commuters herding in to the city centre, the citizens of Hong Kong make every minute count. Used to living in a densely populated community, they have devised strategies for being alone in a crowded place. No British politeness on the MTR commuter railway at 7:30AM: if you want a seat, you fight for it, and those who stand back to let others off are carried away in the rush.

The day starts around 8. Business takes precedence until the lunch hour, when the serious task of eating reasserts itself. Everyone either orders in or eats out in a restaurant or hawker center, where street vendors serve savoury fare *al fresco*. In restaurants, food is whirled to the table and whirled away again as soon as it's eaten, making ready for the next person. Orders are yelled, little slips of paper designate the order, and tea serves both as refreshment and a rinse for crockery. Back at work, the lights are turned off and staff take a post-prandial snooze. Work often continues until 10 at night, especially for shop assistants. The evening rush hour peaks around 7.

The great majority of people live in tiny government-owned flats. Kitchens are minute and ovens a rare luxury; most families eat out in the evening. This is the time for visiting the food markets, where people buy their groceries in tiny amounts, just enough for a day, and for checking out the shops or renting a movie.

While the rest of Hong Kong has an early night, the city is getting into its stride. Karaoke joints, bars and nightclubs go on into the early hours, neon signs flash a welcome to anyone with cash to spend, and Mong Kok brothels do a roaring trade. The huge satellite towns go silent, the KCR (Kowloon–Canton Railway) stops running, and the province gives itself up to the night workers preparing the city for tomorrow.

HONG KONG IN FIGURES

CULTURE AND RECREATION

- Hong Kong's 6 million people squeeze into just 1,000sq km
- 80 per cent of Hong Kong's territory is rural or country park
- 40 per cent of the land is conserved in country parks (the highest ratio in the world)
- The world's largest indoor Chinese restaurant is the Ocean City Restaurant, which can cater for more than 6,000 guests
- The world's largest floating restaurants (the Jumbo and the Sea Palace) are in Aberdeen Harbour on the south side of Hong Kong Island
- Seven of the world's ten busiest McDonald's restaurants are in Hong Kong

ECONOMICS AND SOCIETY

- Under the Sino-British Joint Declaration, Hong Kong retains its existing social and economic system for at least 50 years
- Hong Kong is the world's leading exporter of watches, clothing and imitation jewellery
- Hong Kong is Asia's leading gold distribution centre and third largest gold bullion market

WORLD RECORDS

- More than half of the city's 6 million inhabitants live in public housing (a world record)
- Over 9 million books are borrowed from Hong Kong's public libraries every year (one of the world's highest per capita readerships)
- Despite being the third most densely populated place on Earth, only Sweden and Japan have lower infant and child death rates
- At 111m x 19m, the advertising sign for Nanfang Pharmaceutical Factory's "999" traditional Chinese medicine is the world's largest neon sign. With over 13km of neon tubing, it took half a year to construct

LEADING CONSUMERS

- Hong Kong is per capita the world's leading consumer of oranges
- Hong Kong is per capita the world's leading consumer of cognac
- Hong Kong has the highest per capita ownership of Rolls Royce cars in the world
- Hong Kong has the highest ratio of cafés and restaurants to population in the world

A CHRONOLOGY

4000 BC	Early settlements left some pottery, stone tools and iron implements. Then for many centuries the islands had more pirates than farmers
AD 25	An approximate date for the Han Dynasty Lei Cheng Uk Tomb in Kowloon (► 35). The Chinese Empire had been unified a couple of hundred years earlier, and for the next millennium and a half the area around Hong Kong Island was ruled by a governor based in Canton (Guangzhou) to the north
1685	Canton was opened to European trade, and British and French merchants began to deal in tea and silk. The British later started to import opium as a way of extending their power and profits. Two early traders were William Jardine and James Matheson, both from Scotland
1841	Chinese attempts to block the import of opium ended in their defeat; the treaty concluding the first Opium War ceded Hong Kong Island to the British 'in perpetuity'. Within two decades another treaty conceded the Kowloon Peninsula, again 'in perpetuity'
1898	A further treaty, in 1898, leased substantial land north of Kowloon – the New Territories – to Britain for 99 years
1937–45	Throughout 1937 hundreds of thousands of Chinese, displaced by the Japanese invasion of China, sought refuge in Hong Kong. On 8 December 1941 Japanese aircraft bombed Kowloon, and by Christmas Day the British had surrendered. Over 2,000 people died and 10,000 soldiers were taken prisoner. British civilians were incarcerated in Stanley Prison. With the surrender of the Japanese in August 1945, Hong Kong again became a British colony
1947–67	The years around the 1949 Communist victory in China saw further refugee influxes. The population doubled within 14 years, and when the United States imposed sanctions against China during the Korean War (1950–53) the

colony developed a manufacturing base of its own. China periodically called for the return of its land. In 1962 over 70,000 Chinese flooded across the border

1967 The political passions rocking China during its Cultural Revolution spilled over into Hong Kong in the form of riots and strikes, and the colony seemed on the brink of a premature closure of its lease. But by the end of the year normality returned

1975 100,000 refugees from Vietnam arrived

1982 The British Prime Minister Margaret Thatcher went to Beijing to discuss the colony's future with Deng Xiaoping. The 99-year lease applied only to the New Territories, but China made no secret of its wish to be reunited with all of Hong Kong

1984–88 The Sino-British Joint Declaration in 1984 confirmed the return of the colony to China. In 1988 Beijing published its Basic Law for Hong Kong citizens, guaranteeing their rights

1989 The Tiananmen Square massacre in June served only to confirm Hong Kong's worst fears about the future under China's sovereignty. Over a million people took to the streets in an unprecedented protest against Beijing. The stock market fell over 20 per cent in one day

1997 'The Handover'. On 1 July Hong Kong became a Special Administrative Region of China. English remains an official language. People from other parts of China require special approval for entry

1998 Jan–Feb: an outbreak of potentially lethal 'chicken flu' in humans led to the slaughter of millions of hens throughout the territory
Jul: a new international airport, source of dispute between the UK and China, opened after almost ten years of land reclamation and reconstruction

11

PEOPLE & EVENTS FROM HISTORY

Chris Patten, last British governor of Hong Kong

The 14K and the Bamboo Union

The names of the Triad Secret Societies may sound intriguing but the reality of triad life is a sordid tale. Disaffected youths of both sexes are lured into these secret societies, which control organised crime in Hong Kong, by the promise of easy money and social acceptance. Unless they leave very soon, they are drawn into an organisation with a lifetime membership. After the Communists took control in China in 1949 the triads there were ruthlessly smashed. The jury is still out on how well they fare in post-handover Hong Kong.

CHRIS PATTEN

The last British governor of Hong Kong was its most controversial. Patten was given the job of governor after unexpectedly losing his parliamentary seat in the British elections of 1992. At first his appointment seemed auspicious: he looked like a jolly sort of chap, and his name in Chinese implied good luck. However, he soon caused consternation by establishing a democratic Hong Kong Assembly. This was a controversial step, provoking the Chinese negotiators into refusing to see him and drawing attention to previous British administrations that had never felt any need to govern Hong Kong democratically. Patten was called a serpent, a prostitute and other uncomplimentary names but, casting caution to the wind, he persisted in giving Hong Kong citizens, for the first time, the right to elect representatives to the Assembly. The Chinese threatened to renege on any outstanding contracts after the handover, which endangered and slowed up the new airport projects. But things settled down to a quiet seethe, Patten and family were to be seen at functions all over the territory, and when the final day came they acquitted themselves well.

THE HANDOVER

At midnight on 30 June 1997 Britain's last vestige of empire was handed back to the Chinese. Trepidation surrounded the occasion as people speculated over the intentions of the Chinese authorities and the possible reaction on the part of the Hong Kong population. In the event, it was a muted affair and took place in one of the worst rainstorms in memory. Few people were on the streets, the Patten family and Prince Charles quietly and tearfully slipped away on the royal yacht *Britannia* (her last official job) and the Red Army silently drove across the border to take up their new homes on the island. The expatriate workers who had not chosen to leave celebrated in bars in Lan Kwai Fong, and everyone woke up the next day a little nervously, wondering how their lives would be changed, and a little shocked that nothing seemed to be different.

HONG KONG
how to organise your time

13

ITINERARIES

You can see the essential sights of Hong Kong in just four days. The city, on Hong Kong Island, is compact and can be covered in a day; Kowloon's museums and shops deserve a day's attention; you can tour the southern side of Hong Kong Island another day; and try to visit an outlying island.

WHEN TO GO	The Kowloon trip can be reserved for a rainy day as much of it is under cover, while Lantau really needs good weather since all your time is spent outdoors. The museums close only on the major public holidays, and Chinese New Year in particular. Visit the jade market in the early afternoon as it tends to close down around 3PM.
ITINERARY ONE	HONG KONG ISLAND: THE CITY
Morning	An early morning trip to the Peak (➤ 27), then visit Sheung Wan (➤ 17), with its snake restaurants and medicine shops
Afternoon	The Botanical Gardens (➤ 32) and Hong Kong Park (➤ 37) make a quiet break
Evening	Lan Kwai Fong, the trendy *gweilo* area
ITINERARY TWO	HONG KONG ISLAND: THE SOUTH SHORE
Morning	Stanley (➤ 48) is reached by a spectacular double-decker bus ride. Spend a morning at the beach or browsing around the market stalls
Lunch	At one of the floating restaurants in Aberdeen Harbour (➤ 33)
Afternoon	Explore the sights of Aberdeen
Evening	Causeway Bay; plenty of bars (➤ 83) and restaurants (➤ 62–69), as well as a space-age shopping centre at Times Square (➤ 57)
ITINERARY THREE	LANTAU ISLAND
Morning	An idyllic hour-long boat trip past a sea of moored ships, tiny islands and colourful catamarans ends at Lantau Island. Visit Po Lin

Monastery, where the huge Buddha statue dominates the landscape, see the spectacular temples and tea gardens, and walk a little way along the Lantau Trail

Lunch

In Tai O, the tiny fishing village on stilts

Afternoon

Sightseeing in Tai O

Evening

Lantau's Discovery Bay and its rocking nightlife, followed by a starlit journey back to the city

ITINERARY FOUR

KOWLOON

Morning

Kowloon Park to see *t'ai chi ch'uan* exercises and to visit the Hong Kong Museum of History (► 39). The Museum of Art (► 43) and Space Museum (► 42) are both near by in the Hong Kong Cultural Centre on the waterfront

Afternoon

Prowl around Kowloon's shops. Catch the jade market at Temple Street before it closes (► 41) and squeeze in a trip to the Lei Cheng Uk Museum (► 35) or Wong Tai Sin Temple (► 46)

Evening

Take a trip down one of the night markets (► 41) and then dine *al fresco* on seafood at a market restaurant

Buddha statue, Po Lin Monastery, Lantau Island

WALKS

THE SIGHTS

- Bowen Road shrines
- Mid Levels
- Lover's Stone Garden
- Police Museum (➤ 59)
- Covered market
- Meat and fish stalls along Wan Chai Road

INFORMATION

Distance 3km
Time 2 hours
Start point Bowen Road
🚩 G10
🚌 Bus 15 from Central Bus Terminal or Peak Terminal; get off at the Adventist Hospital at the horseshoe bend where Bowen Road meets Stubbs Road
End point Johnston Road
🚩 F8
🚋 Wan Chai
🚌 Tram stop on Johnston Road

ALONG THE QUIET MID LEVELS OF THE PEAK, THEN INTO HECTIC WAN CHAI

Shady and quiet, Bowen Road runs along the Mid Levels on Hong Kong Island, an area of housing half-way up Victoria Peak; note the small roadside shrines. After walking west for 15 minutes, look for steps on the left up to an exposed rock shrine (Lover's Stone Garden) via a small complex of incense-burning pots. Continue along Bowen Road as far as Wan Chai Gap Road. A detour can be made left, to Stubbs Road and the Police Museum, but the main walk goes right, down steep Wan Chai Gap Road. At the bottom, turn right on to Kennedy Road and then left on to Queen's Road East. Turn right at the covered market on to bustling Wan Chai Road.

Turn left on to Johnston Road; pause to enjoy traditional herbal tea at No. 137, next to the Simsons Commercial Building. For lunch, try Indian cuisine at the International Curry House on Tai Wong Street East, or at the Jo Jo Mess Club (➤ 66), entered on Lee Tung Street, both left turns off Johnston Road.

One block to the south is Hennessy Road, where there are plenty of fast-food eateries.

Fish stall in Wan Chai Road

THE HEART OF HONG KONG

Start this walk at Western Market, once the local wet, or fresh food, market, opposite Macau Ferry Pier on Hong Kong Island; built in 1906 and renovated in 1991, it is now an arts and crafts centre. Head south, uphill, then turn right into Wing Lok Street, a traditional trading street with neon signs, ageing buildings and a variety of flourishing trades. Turning back along Bonham Strand West, notice the flashy new ginseng wholesalers still hung with huge traditional lanterns and painted signboards.

Inspect the food on sale in Sheung Wan Market; for an adventure, visit the top floor and sample some local dishes. Along Bonham Strand East and Queen's Road there are many antiques stores and shops selling calligraphy materials, wedding clothes and funeral paraphernalia.

At Peel Street, turn uphill and wander through the street market, which sells all manner of things foreign. Turn right into Hollywood Road and admire the applied arts shops that fill this part of Sheung Wan. The Man Mo Temple is on this road; turn right down Ladder Street, which will take you to more antiques, curios and junk merchants in Upper Lascar Row. From here, go downhill to return to the walk's starting point, taking in on the way Possession Street, where the British flag was first raised.

THE SIGHTS

- Western Market
- Bonham Strand West ginseng traders (➤ 29)
- Sheung Wan Market
- Bonham Strand East antiques shops (➤ 29)
- Man Mo Temple (➤ 30)
- Possession Street

INFORMATION

Distance 3km
Time 2 hours
Start and end point Western Market
🚇 D7
🚉 Sheung Wan
🚃 Any tram from Central

Antiques shop

EVENING STROLLS

THE SIGHTS

- Star Ferry (➤ 38)
- Chinese garden
- Harbour views
- Central Plaza (➤ 50)
- Streets of Wan Chai

INFORMATION

Distance 1.2km
Time 30 minutes
Start point Wan Chai Star Ferry
➕ F8
🚇 Wan Chai
End point Wan Chai MTR
➕ F8
🚇 Wan Chai
🚋 Trams to Causeway Bay and Sheung Wan

THE SIGHTS

- Clock Tower
- Hong Kong Cultural Centre (➤ 51)
- Space Museum (➤ 42)
- Museum of Art (➤ 43)
- Harbour views

INFORMATION

Distance 1.5km
Time 30 minutes
Start point Star Ferry Terminal, Tsim Sha Tsui, Kowloon
➕ F7
End point Kowloon Railway Terminus
➕ G6
🚌 Buses and taxis are plentiful

Clock tower outside Star Ferry terminal

THE ELEVATED WALKWAY OF WAN CHAI

From the Wan Chai Star Ferry terminal on Hong Kong Island, take the walkway to find the red China Resources Building (CRB). Below it, and worth a visit, is a Chinese garden. East of the CRB is the Museum of Chinese Historical Relics, made to look like an ancient Chinese building and containing some interesting displays. Retracing your steps takes you past an excellent Chinese products emporium and through the Hong Kong Convention and Exhibition Centre where you can admire some harbour views. The overhead walk continues through the splendid Central Plaza and the Immigration Tower, and across some of the seedier streets of old Wan Chai. End your stroll at the Wan Chai MTR station.

WATERFRONT PROMENADE OF TSIM SHA TSUI

Outside Star Ferry terminal in Tsim Sha Tsui, Kowloon, is the Clock Tower, all that is left of the Old Kowloon Railway Station, built in 1916 and demolished in 1978. Pass two highly controversial structures: the windowless Hong Kong Cultural Centre and, across the road, the central extension of the Peninsula Hotel. Most of the other hotels along this stretch of road are equally unattractive,

so walk to the back of the Hong Kong Space Museum and the Hong Kong Museum of Art. Stroll along the Waterfront Promenade and enjoy glittering night views of Wan Chai and Causeway Bay across the harbour. Rejoin Salisbury Road and continue east as far as the underpass, where you can either turn back or continue to the railway terminus at Hung Hom.

ORGANISED SIGHTSEEING

HONG KONG TOURIST ASSOCIATION (HKTA ➤ 88–9) conducts a number of interesting tours:

- The half-day Heritage Tour to the New Territories is recommended, as is the more comprehensive whole-day tour.
- The 'Land Between' Tour includes a temple, street market and fishing village in the New Territories.
- Horse-racing Tour to either Happy Valley or Sha Tin racecourse (September–June).
- Family Insight Tour includes a visit, with a translator, to a temple and a local home on a public housing estate.
- Sports and Recreation Tour.

TOURIST ENTERPRISES ☎ 2368 0647 runs a whole-day tour of Hong Kong Island, including Aberdeen and Stanley. They also offer a *dim sum* lunch on the Jumbo floating restaurant. There is also an evening open-top bus tour and harbour cruise.

WATER TOURS ☎ 2367 1970 and **STAR FERRY** ☎ 2366 7024/2324 also conduct harbour cruises, and Water Tours has other cruises, including a sampan ride around Aberdeen.

GRAYLINE TOURS ☎ 2368 7111 conducts city tours and dinner cruises, and also runs day trips to China.

Heritage tour highlight

The Man Mo Temple in Tai Po (➤ 30), part of the HKTA's Heritage Tour, is an especially rich experience on a Saturday, when the surrounding street market is buzzing with life. The ancient grey stone temple, dedicated to the gods of war and literature, offers a calm respite from the hurly burly of the market outside. In the market, look out for snakes in the snake soup shops, partially dissected live fish on the fish stalls and old ladies carrying their wares suspended from a pole across their shoulders.

Sampan ride round Aberdeen Harbour

19

EXCURSIONS

INFORMATION

Lamma Island
Distance 10km
Journey time 50 minutes
🚢 Ferry from Central Pier,
Central ➕ F

LAMMA ISLAND

This island, with a chic, radical, and bohemian image created by its resident expatriate community, offers refuge from the concrete jungle as well as genuine glimpses of a fast-disappearing rural lifestyle. Surprisingly good meals can be enjoyed at either of the two ferry villages – Yung Shue Wan and Sok Kwu Wan – and the hour-long walk between them takes in a decent beach and scenic viewpoints. In Yung Shue Wan there are a number of craft shops worth browsing around.

Hakka women cutting watercress, New Territories

NEW TERRITORIES

The New Territories are best explored via the Kowloon–Canton Railway (KCR ► 91). From Kowloon station the line heads northwards, passing a number of interesting stopping points along the way. From either Tai Po Market station or Tai Wo station, take a taxi to the Hong Kong Railway Museum and visit the Man Mo Temple, Tai Po, in the adjacent pedestrianised market street. At the next station (Fanling) take the right exit; the Taoist Ying Sin Kwun Temple just across the road is worth a visit, as is the old village just minutes from the next station (Sheung Shui). Take the overhead footway to the right and head down to the bus station. With McDonald's on your right, walk along the main road until you see the old lanes on the left. Life here, only a couple of miles south of the border, is little different from that in the rest of China.

New Territories
Distance Tai Po 25km; Sheung Shui 35km
Journey time 1 hour
🚇 MTR from any station to Kowloon Tong ➕ F2, where the interchange accesses equally regular KCR trains travelling north to Lo Wu. The last stop is Sheung Shui, less than an hour from Central, which is as far as you can go without travelling on into China.

Hong Kong Railway Museum
🕐 Wed–Mon 9–4. Closed Tue

MACAU

Cobbled streets, baroque architecture and the traditional cuisine of Portugal's last colony are good reasons for taking the trip to Macau, scheduled to revert to China in December 1999. Macau is compact and most of the main places of interest can be covered in a day; highlights include the ruined façade of 17th-century St Paul's Church, the Jesuit Monte Fortress, and a number of old churches and temples. Hotels and good restaurants are easy to find, and prices are agreeably lower than those in Hong Kong.

THE PEOPLE'S REPUBLIC OF CHINA

Shenzen is designated by the Beijing government as a Special Economic Zone, which means that tourists, investors – anyone with money to spend – is welcomed with open arms. Splendid China is a theme park with the Great Wall, the Forbidden City and other monuments of Chinese architecture reduced to one-fifthteenth real size. The nearby China Folk Culture village introduces the country's ethnic minorities.

Guangzhou (Canton) on the Pearl River, is a major city and port, and has been trading with Europeans for 400 years. It offers an astonishing food market, a fascinating royal tomb from 100 BC, several temples and bustling street life.

INFORMATION

Macau
Distance 60km
Journey time 1 hour by jetfoil
🚢 Jetfoil from the Shun Tak Centre
🚇 D7
✉ 200 Connaught Road, a ten-minute walk west of Central
🎫 Jetfoil: HK$119
ℹ Tourist office in Macau:
✉ Largo do Senado, Edificio Ritz No 9
☎ (853) 315 566
Tourist office in Hong Kong:
✉ Shop 336, Shun Tak Centre, 200 Connaught Road, Central
☎ 2857 2287
❓ Take your passport; no visa required for Europeans or North Americans

The People's Republic of China
Shenzen can be seen in a day, while Guangzhou (Canton) is best enjoyed with an overnight stay

Shenzen
Distance 40km
Journey time 40 minutes
🚈 KCR from Kowloon Tong station to border at Lo Wo
❓ Organised tours: Grayline Tours ☎ 2368 7111

Guangzhou (Canton)
Distance 120km
Journey time Under 3 hours by train
❓ Express train from Hong Kong
❓ Organised tours: Grayline Tours ☎ 2368 7111

St Paul's, Macau

WHAT'S ON

For details, look for the free fortnightly *Hong Kong Magazine* and the Hong Kong Tourist Association's weekly *Hong Kong Diary*. The English newspapers also carry details of events (► 92).

Chinese Lunar festivals are movable; dates are given below for the years 1999 and 2000.

FEBRUARY	*Chinese (Lunar) New Year* (16–18 Feb 1999; 4–6 Feb 2000): essentially a family event. The week before the New Year is intensely busy and crowded; the harbour fireworks display is magnificent, but the crowds are enormous.
MID-JANUARY– MID-MARCH	*Arts Festival:* international orchestral, dance, and theatre events over three to four weeks throughout the territory
LATE MARCH–APRIL	*International Film Festival:* for two weeks; various venues
MAY	*Tin Hau Festival* (10 May 1999; 27 Apr 2000): a 12th-century legend, about a girl who saves her brothers from drowning, is celebrated in the Tin Hau temples (► 53). Decorated fishing junks and temples; Chinese street operas held near the temples
	Birthday of Lord Buddha (22 May 1999; 11 May 2000): at temples throughout the territory; Buddha's statue is ceremonially bathed and scented (► 45), symbolising the washing away of sins and material encumbrances
JUNE	*Dragon Boat Festival* (18 Jun 1999; 6 Jun 2000): the colourful and noisy dragon-boat races are held and rice dumplings eaten to commemorate the political protests of a 4th-century poet/patriot Chu Yuan
SEPTEMBER	*Mid-Autumn Festival* (24 Sep 1999; 12 Sep 2000): families head out with lanterns, and eat mooncakes to commemorate a 14th-century uprising against the Mongols
OCTOBER–NOVEMBER	*Festival of Asian Arts:* (even-numbered years only) Asian music, dance and theatre

HONG KONG's
top 25 sights

The sights are shown on the maps on the inside front cover and inside back cover, numbered **1–25** *from west to east across the city*

AIRPORT CORE PROGRAMME EXHIBITION

HIGHLIGHTS

- Ferry ride to Tsuen Wan
- Double-decker ride past public beaches
- View of the bridge
- Model of the airport site

DID YOU KNOW?

- The bridge extends 2.2km
- The suspension section of the bridge is 1,377m long

INFORMATION

- 🔛 Off map to west
- ✉ 401 Castle Peak Road, Ting Kau, New Territories
- ☎ 2491 902
- 🕐 Tue–Fri 10–5; Sat, Sun 10–6:30. Closed Mon and public holidays
- 🚉 Tsuen Wan
- 🚢 Hoverferry from Central pier to Tsuen Wan (journey time approx ½ hour)
- 🚌 53 double-decker from Tsuen Wan ferry pier; 243B minibus; Tsuen Wan MTR 96 minibus
- 🅿 Free
- ❓ The Lantau Link Exhibition on Tsing Yi Island offers further views and information
- ↔ Sam Tung Uk Museum (► 25)

The opening of the Tsing Ma Bridge, linking Lantau Island to the mainland

24

Hong Kong's new airport at Chek Lap Kok, built on reclaimed land, constitutes the world's biggest civil engineering project ever. The exhibition graphically chronicles the whole vast enterprise, and the journey to it from Central by ferry and bus is an experience in itself.

The coastal journey Take the hoverferry from Central up to Tsuen Wan for a truly exhilarating journey through the world's busiest seaway, quite literally dodging past all manner of seacraft. From the ferry pier at Tsuen Wan a No. 53 double-decker bus runs along the coastal Castle Peak road, built in 1919, to the exhibition centre. From the top deck of the bus there are excellent views south and westwards of the coastline and building projects. The old airport at Kai Tak was hopelessly small, as well as being dangerously situated in a built-up area, and the new airport is determined not to make the same mistakes.

The exhibition The exhibition centre itself is about an hour's fascinating viewing, with models of the ten building projects in the 'core programme', plus photographs of the various stages of the reclamation, videos and slide shows. From the centre there is a panoramic view of the Tsing Ma Bridge and some of the building projects. These include the levelling of tiny Chek Lap Kok island and a neighbouring island, and the reclamation of the shallow waters around them to create an island about 3¼ miles long and 2 miles wide (moving the equivalent in volume of 325 Empire State Buildings in the process). The bridge is the world's longest and heaviest road and rail suspension bridge. Other ongoing projects include a new town, the new harbour crossing, eight new hotels along the route of the rail link, and a HK$200 billion hotel at the airport.

SAM TUNG UK MUSEUM

The clean, simple lines of this ancient Hakka dwelling are set off against the surrounding forest of high-rise housing blocks. The quality of life of those who once lived here might be compared favourably with that of the people of today perched up in their tiny claustrophobic apartments.

History Around a million people now live in Tsuen Wan, which until as recently as 1977 was a sleepy little village of a few thousand souls. Back in the 17th century this area was subject to constant attacks from the sea by pirates, and so the inhabitants built walled villages to act as a defence. Within each village lived the members of a single clan, in the case of Sam Tung Uk a Hakka clan called the Chans. The Hakka, originally from the north of China, moved to southern China in the 12th and 13th centuries. Feuds over land tenure led some Hakka clans to migrate further, to Hong Kong, Taiwan and Singapore. The village was probably built in 1786.

What to see The museum is a complete walled village consisting of three connected halls that formed the core of village life. The name Sam Tung Uk means 'three-beam dwelling', since the three rows of houses were supported by three central beams called *tung*. The main ancestral hall is at the front and its design is highly ornate; its original decorations have been restored to their bright reds and greens. The other two halls are more rustic in nature, as befits their simpler role as centres for the clan's daily living. These halls now contain displays of farming equipment, furniture of the period and kitchen utensils. Outside are a fish pond, a threshing floor and the gatehouse that guarded the village.

HIGHLIGHTS

- Ancestral hall with ornate, highly coloured decorations
- Landscaped gardens
- Orientation room
- Blackwood furniture
- Cooking equipment
- Gatehouse of walled village
- Fish ponds
- Threshing floor

INFORMATION

- ✚ Off map to north
- ✉ Kwu Uk Lane, Tsuen Wan, New Territories
- ☎ 2411 2001
- 🕐 Mon, Wed–Sun 9–4
- 🚇 Tsuen Wan
- 🚌 Bus 51 from Tai Ho Road North takes you to the hoverferry back to Central
- ♿ Few
- 🎫 Free
- ❓ HKTA Heritage tour (➤ 19), plus private tours
- ↔ Airport Core Programme Exhibition Centre (➤ 24)

UNIVERSITY MUSEUM

INFORMATION

- B8
- 94 Bonham Road, Hong Kong Island
- 2859 2114
- Mon–Sat 9:30–6. Closed public holidays and 16 March
- Sheung Wan
- Bus 3 from Rumsey Street in Central or 23 from North Point ferry terminal
- None
- Free

This is an interesting little collection of artefacts, predominantly Chinese, and is well worth the effort required to get out to see it. It is in the Fung Ping Shan Building, in the peaceful University of Hong Kong campus at the end of Bonham Road, and usually blessedly empty.

Nestorian bronze crosses The displays in this out-of-the-way museum date from the 5th century BC onwards, but the highlight of the collection is a set of 467 Nestorian bronze crosses – the largest such collection in the world – which belonged to members of a Christian sect that originated in Syria and came to China during the Tang Dynasty (AD 618–906). The crosses date back to the Yuan Dynasty (1280–1367) and were probably worn as part of a belt or as a pendant. They are made in various cross shapes from swastikas to regular crucifixes and birds.

Other exhibits Notable among the other bronze items on display are mirrors from the Warring States period (475–221 BC), and Shang and Zhou ritual vessels and weapons. The museum also houses an enormous collection of ceramics dating back as far as neolithic times. The painted neolithic pottery is very fine, and a Han Dynasty horse is full of life. Look out for the three-colour glaze Tang pottery, the famous kiln wares of Song and both polychrome and monochrome ceramics from the Ming and Qing Dynasties.

There are collections of artefacts from other Asian countries, including some Indian Buddhist sculptures and items from Thailand, Vietnam and Korea. Scroll paintings, inlaid blackwood furniture and a huge bronze drum make up the rest of the collection.

4

VICTORIA PEAK

Visiting the Peak is one of the first things you should do when you get to Hong Kong. The hilltop views are spectacular and the area offers some peaceful, shady walks. Be sure to visit on a clear day.

Head for heights Some people like to make the pilgrimage up the Peak twice – during the day and again at night, when the full majesty of the city below is spelled out in lights. The Peak is a relatively unspoilt oasis in a concrete jungle, home of the rich and famous and a good place for a quiet walk or even a strenuous jog.

Top stop For visitors there is the Peak Galleria, a veritable tourist trap. Feeding dollars into one of the telescopes is worth the money on a clear day, while the Odditorium (400 displays of strange-but-true facts and artefacts), simulated rides, and restaurants in the Peak Tower offer further distractions. The trip up in the Peak Tram (constructed 1888) is good fun as long as you don't have to queue up for it for hours – for a start, avoid weekends and the first day after a misty spell. Whatever you do, do not forget your camera. From the tram stop you could walk along Mount Austin Road to Victoria Park Gardens and the ruins of the Governor's Lodge, destroyed by the Japanese in World War II.

HIGHLIGHTS

- Views over Hong Kong
- Tram ride to the top
- Old Governor's Lodge, with toposcope in its gardens
- Souvenirs in Peak Galleria
- Outdoor tables in Peak Café
- Green-arrowed walk up Mount Austin Road

INFORMATION

- ✚ C9/D9
- ✉ Peak Tower, Peak Road
- 🕐 Peak Tram: runs 7AM—midnight
  Odditorium: 9AM—10PM
- 🍴 Peak Galleria (snacks) and Peak Café (££)
- 🚃 Trams run every 10–15 minutes from terminals at Garden Road and Cotton Tree Drive.
  Central Bus 15 from Central Bus Terminal to Victoria Gap.
  Minibus 1 from HMS *Tamar*
- ♿ Good
- 🎫 Tram fare: moderate
  Peak Tower: free
  Odditorium: moderate
- ↔ Botanical & Zoological Gardens (► 32),
  Hong Kong Park (► 37)

Souvenir shopping in the Peak Galleria

27

5

TAI PING SHAN STREET

HIGHLIGHTS

- Views down alleyways leading to Des Voeux Road
- Street temples with gold-painted doorway carvings
- Shops and stalls around temples
- Hollywood Garden
- Church in shopping block

INFORMATION

- ✚ C8
- ✉ Tai Ping Shan Street, Sheung Wan
- 🕐 Temples: daily 8–8
- 🍴 Cooked food stalls in nearby Sheung Wan Market
- 🚇 Sheung Wan
- 🚋 Trams run to Western Market from Central, Wan Chai and Causeway Bay
- ♿ Access difficult because of steep steps
- 💰 Temples: free, but donations appreciated
- ↔ Bonham Strand East and West (➤ 29)

In many ways this street symbolises much of what life is like for Hong Kong's ordinary citizens. At the eastern end are crowded apartment blocks; at the western end some of the mystery of old Hong Kong lurks in the peculiar little temples.

Backstreet buildings South of Hollywood Road and its tourist-hungry antiques and curio shops lies Tai Ping Shan Street, a quiet backwater of crumbling 1950s flats, car-repair workshops and narrow-stepped alleys that lead north through street markets. At the western end, what seems to be a dead end turns into another narrow-stepped alley with tiny temples on either side.

Temple life Inside the street temples the atmosphere is somewhat less than pious, with people shaking their fortunes out of bamboo pots to have them read by interpreters, visitors bringing offerings of thanks, and others just lounging about passing the time of day. Like most temples in Hong Kong, these ones like to hedge their bets by paying homage to the Buddhist pantheon as well as to Taoist gods. Nothing here is in English, so you can be sure these are serious, working temples where a woman may come to ask for children or seek promotion at work.

Carving over temple door

Chinese religion is essentially pragmatic; if the gods turn up the goods then they must be paid. Around the temple are stalls selling things the gods appreciate, such as joss sticks, incense candles, paper figures and fake paper or 'hell' money to be burned and sent up in smoke to the dead to spend in the next world.

BONHAM STRAND EAST AND WEST

The best time to visit Bonham Strand is in the winter, when the Chinese believe in consuming strong, hearty food. A typical dish, whose main ingredient is very evident in the cages along Bonham Strand East, is warming, strengthening snake soup, liver-coloured, thick, and meaty in texture and taste.

Bonham Strand East The eastern section of Bonham Strand is full of cafés and shops that sell outrageous dishes such as snake's gall bladder wine and snake soup. If you wait around you will be able to watch the victims being chosen and skinned on the pavement before they are put into the cooking pot. The snakes (and a few other creatures that shouldn't be here at all) await their fate in cages on the pavement. In some shops lizards and turtles sit alongside cobras, pythons and various other deadly creatures. The deadlier the snake, the more powerful its medicinal value is believed to be. What many people find shocking is not the snakes, sitting in their cages, but the customers who drink the soup itself.

Bonham Strand West You reach the western half of Bonham Strand after a brief sortie into Wing Lok Street. Ginseng wholesalers share the road here with some prosperous-looking banks. Most of the quaint old wooden interiors of the former have now given way to glass and chrome, but the jars of unidentifiable items are still there. Ginseng is an expensive commodity and much wheeler-dealing goes on over its price. Different types of ginseng bring different prices, the American variety being the cheapest while ginseng from Korea and China is considered more efficacious and is therefore more expensive.

HIGHLIGHTS

- Snake shop at No. 127 Bonham Strand East
- Ginseng wholesalers on Bonham Strand West
- Chinese medicine shops in Ko Shing Street
- Street barbers in Sutherland Street
- Nearby Possession Street, marking the place where Hong Kong was claimed by the British
- Sheung Wan Market

INFORMATION

- ✚ D7
- ✉ Bonham Strand, Sheung Wan
- 🕙 Shops close on public holidays, particularly Chinese New Year
- 🍴 Food stalls in Sheung Wan Market and streets around Bonham Strand (£); fast food near MTR station (£)
- 🚇 Sheung Wan
- 🚌 Trams stop at Western Market and go on through Central to Causeway Bay
- ♿ Good
- 🆓 Free
- ↔ Tai Ping Shan Street (► 28) Man Mo Temple (► 30)

MAN MO TEMPLE

The most remarkable aspects of this tiny, crumbling temple are the vast and increasingly weatherworn and grubby apartment towers that loom up all around it. Notwithstanding, the interior of the temple is very atmospheric, and coils of incense hanging from the ceiling evoke a suitably spiritual mood.

HIGHLIGHTS

- Statues of Man Cheong and Kuan Ti
- Sedan chairs once used to carry statues
- Embroideries surrounding statues
- Drum and bell on right of entrance door
- Soot-blackened deities on left of entrance door
- Gold and brass standards carried during parades
- Resident fortune-tellers

INFORMATION

- D8
- Junction of Hollywood Road and Ladder Street
- Daily 7–5
- Sheung Wan
- Access difficult
- Free
- Tai Ping Shan Street (► 28)
  Bonham Strand East and West (► 29)

Interior The temple represents an eclectic mix of Taoism and Buddhism, both of which have many adherents in Hong Kong. Two gods share the temple: Man, or Man Cheong, the god of literature; and Mo, or Kuan Ti, the god of war. A casual ambience prevails – cats wander about, some people have their fortunes told using bamboo sticks, other visitors offer fruit or incense sticks to the gods. The statues of Man and Mo themselves are dressed lavishly in the most beautifully embroidered outfits. By the door are the figures of some lesser deities, while beside the two main statues in the temple are representations of Pao Kung, the god of justice, and Shing Wong, the god who protects this region of the city. A drum and a gong are sounded whenever an offering is made to the gods.

Nearby sights Next door, to the right, is the Litt Shing Kung, or All Saints Temple, where you can see people consulting the resident soothsayers who interpret the *chim* (bamboo sticks with numbers on) tipped out of the bamboo pots. The room to the left of the temple was once used as a schoolroom where free education was offered to the children of poor Chinese families. Outside the temple, the building to its right across Ladder Street was used in the 1950s film *The World of Suzie Wong*.

8

CENTRAL MARKET

To appreciate fully just how different life is in Hong Kong, visit one of the places where most people do their food shopping. Central Market sells some outrageous items, and the odour alone will send you scuttling back to the supermarket.

Layout This is one of the biggest fresh food, or 'wet', markets in Hong Kong, and you should visit it early, as most of the business is completed by mid-morning. The layout of the building is very organised, with chicken and fish on one floor, red meats on another, and fruit and vegetables on yet another. There are about 300 stallholders in the market, and the stock includes such peculiar items as salamanders and sea cucumbers.

What to look for Turtles are slaughtered to order – an especially gruesome sight – and other gory executions can be observed on the fish stalls. Scrotums are a delicacy sold in the meat hall, alongside tongues, intestines, ears and chicken feet (said to be especially good if cooked in mustard). Look out for lotus root on the lower floors, a common vegetable which can be recognised by its resemblance to Swiss cheese. In autumn and winter a peculiar smell might rise above the odours wafting up from down-stairs. This is not caused by a gas leak, but comes from the huge, spiky durian fruits stacked up on the fruit stalls – they have a flavour that is a cross between garlic and custard; it is most assuredly an acquired taste!

HIGHLIGHTS

- Old-fashioned delivery bicycles on ground floor
- Fresh fish and live chickens awaiting slaughter
- Exotic green vegetables
- Strong-smelling durians
- Dried fish products
- Signs on staircases warning people not to sleep
- Hawker stalls on top floor
- Beancurd-product stalls

INFORMATION

- ✚ D8
- ✉ Junction of Queen Victoria Street and Des Voeux Road
- 🕓 Daily 7–10, 5–8
- Ⓢ Central
- 🚃 Trams from Sheung Wan, Wan Chai and Causeway Bay
- 🛳 Ferry from Tsim Sha Tsui
- ♿ None
- 💷 Free
- ↔ Exchange Square (► 34) Statue Square (► 36)

9

BOTANICAL & ZOOLOGICAL GARDENS

HIGHLIGHTS

- Bromeliads, air plants and carnivorous plants
- Amazing variety of butterflies, especially in autumn
- Belly-banded squirrels running free
- Black jaguar
- Orang-utan families
- Tree kangaroos from central New Guinea
- Flamingos
- Local people practising *t'ai chi*

INFORMATION

- ✚ D8
- ✉ Several entrances; from Central the most accessible gate is on Upper Albert Road
- ☎ 2530 0155
- ⏰ Daily 7AM–10PM
- Ⓒ Central
- 🚌 Bus 3 or 12 from Connaught Road
- 🍴 Snack kiosk
- ♿ Good
- 💲 Free
- ↔ Victoria Peak (➤ 27)
  Hong Kong Park (➤ 37)

In the middle of this urban sprawl these gardens form a quiet little haven of peace – even if the small zoo can seem a sad place, with the caged inmates glaring balefully out at you.

Oasis of calm This century-old complex, which once looked out over Victoria Harbour, is enclosed today by the city's towers (and is bisected by a road; use the underpass to get from one part to the other.) The most colourful time here is autumn, not summer; the air filled with the scents of dazzling flowers and the wings of myriad butterflies. There are hundreds of species of birds, many of the rare ones breeding happily in captivity. The greenhouse collection includes bromeliads, air plants and insectivorous plants, such as pitcher plants, Venus fly-traps and rare butterworts. Early in the morning the gardens are full of people performing the slow exercise programme called *t'ai chi ch'uan*, which is designed to get the life forces flowing properly around the body.

Government House Opposite the gardens, on Upper Albert Road, is Government House, where Hong Kong's British governors used to live. The house was built in 1855 and was added to through the years, perhaps one of the most attractive additions being the Japanese tower and roof corners put up during the Occupation. Government House is closed to the public currently, but you can peer in through the gates or, if you are lucky, visit its gardens when they open for two days in March.

Many birds breed in the Gardens

ABERDEEN

What strikes home about Aberdeen, the waterborne neighbourhood of sampans moored along the south side of Hong Kong Island, is the bustling boatlife. Eating, sleeping, making a living – all life goes on in this crowded and lively waterway.

The harbour The district of Aberdeen is one of Hong Kong's top tourist sights. Its main attraction is the harbour, where many people still live on junks and sampans, rarely leaving them to set foot on dry land. Also here are several huge floating seafood restaurants, sights of interest in their own right. There are free ferry-boat rides out to the restaurants and there is no obligation to eat once you get there. It is even more fun to negotiate a price for a sampan ride with one of the old ladies who operate the boats.

Ap Lei Chau In the harbour is the island of Ap Lei Chau, best known for its junk-building. The walk across the bridge to the island offers good views of Aberdeen Harbour. Beneath the bridge are the city's dragon boats, stored away and headless until the next Dragon Boat Festival (▶ 22). There are two Tin Hau temples here, one on the island and one further inland. In Aberdeen Country Park there are many walks and picnic spots.

HIGHLIGHTS

- Traditional boatyards on Ap Lei Chau
- Fishing junks
- Floating restaurants
- Tin Hau temples
- Views of Aberdeen Harbour from Ap Lei Chau Bridge
- Old ladies chartering sampans
- Marina Club

INFORMATION

- ✚ Off map to south
- 🕐 Most restaurants are likely to close on Chinese New Year's Day
- 🍴 Floating restaurants (▶ 62)
- 🚌 Bus 7 or 70 from Central Bus Terminus
- ♿ Few

Sampans in Aberdeen Harbour

33

11

EXCHANGE SQUARE

- Life-sized bronze water buffalo statues
- Oversized statue of *t'ai chi ch'uan* practitioner
- Waterfront
- Land reclamation to the north
- No. 1 Exchange Square

INFORMATION

- ✚ D8
- ✉ Exchange Square, Central
- 🚇 Central
- 🍴 Café in the Forum; also fast food available on lower floors (£)
- ♿ Good

The best times to visit this square and the neighbouring areas are when they are busy: either at lunchtime when the people who work in the area are out foraging for their lunch in the delis and cafés; or on Sunday when the Filipino maids get their day off and picnic on every available spot, networking with their friends.

The scene Exchange Square (designed by Hong Kong's P&T Architects) consists of several ultra-modern tower blocks set on what is, for the moment, the waterfront. Even on the best of days it can be a chilly spot, with winds seemingly always blowing in from the sea and whistling through the gaps between buildings. The towers provide shade, the waterfalls the cooling sound of water, and the statuary a sense of dignity and place. The buildings are huge monoliths of smooth, pink granite, probably quarried from one of Hong Kong's many hills.

Number 1 Have a look inside No. 1 Exchange Square. On the first floor is an exhibition gallery, while the ride up the escalator takes you past another two stunning waterfalls. The overall effect of the square is very bleak, and the lobbies of the buildings would fit well into the next Gotham City movie. The scene is, however, considerably more cheerful on Sundays when the place is full of noise and laughter.

Exchange Square

12

LEI CHENG UK MUSEUM

Though built over an ancient Han dynasty tomb, this little museum is now surrounded by towerblocks and sits right in the thick of the daily lives of thousands of Hong Kong people. This continuity, spanning 2,000 years, between the living and the dead is somehow very moving.

Unique find The Lei Cheng Uk Museum is very modest in its appearance and layout, but it contains Hong Kong's oldest man-made structure. The tomb, built between AD 25 and 220, consists of a central domed chamber with four barrel-roofed side chambers leading from it. (The entrance-way was destroyed before the tomb was noticed.) The tomb was discovered accidentally in 1955 when the housing development around it was being built.

Tomb objects No human remains were found, but inscriptions on the bricks wish goodwill and peace to the region and mark the name Master Xue, perhaps the tomb's occupant or even the brickmaker. What was found were objects the deceased would need in the next life – a cooker, pots and pans, a store of grain and other essential items. This is a custom that still continues today: contemporary necessities such as cash, a video, a television set or a car are made out of paper and then burned at funerals and during the month of the Hungry Ghosts.

The tomb is sealed up for protection and all you can do is peer in at it through the broken entrance porch. None the less it remains a potent image of the past that has survived in Hong Kong for all these years. It is doubtful whether the Hong Kong & Shanghai Banking Corporation building will last as long.

HIGHLIGHTS

- 2,000-year-old Han Dynasty tomb with four side chambers
- Niche at back of chamber for holding funerary urn
- Display room with funerary objects
- Local park, where old men take caged birds for a walk

INFORMATION

- E2
- 41 Tonkin Street, Lei Cheng Uk Estate, Sham Shui Po
- 2386 2863
- Mon–Wed, Fri–Sat 10–1, 2–6; Sun and some public holidays 1–6. Closed Thu, 25–26 Dec and first three days of the Chinese New Year
- Cheung Sha Wan
- Bus 2 from Tonkin Street to Star Ferry
- Good access to museum displays but not to tomb
- Free

13

STATUE SQUARE

HIGHLIGHTS

- Hong Kong & Shanghai Bank Corporation building (➤ 50)
- Old Bank of China building
- Expatriate Filipino gatherings on Sunday
- By-law signs written in English, Chinese and Togalog
- Statue of Sir Thomas Jackson
- Legislative Council Building
- Cenotaph Pier
- Chater Garden
- Interior of Mandarin Oriental Hotel (➤ 80)

INFORMATION

- ✚ E8
- ✉ Statue Square, Central
- 🚇 Central
- 🚊 Trams to Causeway Bay and Sheung Wan
- ♿ Excellent
- 🎫 Free
- ↔ Central Market (➤ 31)
  Star Ferry (➤ 38)

Statue Square is just one section of a whole chain of pleasant open spaces in the heart of the Central district. The space allows for amazing landward views of the surrounding architecture; take care not to get a crick in your neck, peering upwards.

Colonial core This square once formed the heart of colonial Hong Kong Island. Surrounded by 19th-century buildings, its northern edge opened on to the harbour. It is a far cry from that now: its only structure of any age is the Legislative Council Building, previously the Supreme Court. The centrepiece of the square was once the statue of Queen Victoria, which now resides in Victoria Park in Causeway Bay.

Surrounding architecture The square today is overdeveloped to qualify as a green area, with concrete pools and tasteless fountains. Much more important is the outstanding architecture around it (➤ 50). Look for Norman Foster's 1986 Hong Kong & Shanghai Banking Corporation building (walk up to its first floor). Behind and to the east, I M Pei's angular Bank

of China Tower (1985–90) lurches skywards, sending out bad *chi* (➤ 50, panel). More pleasing is the old Bank of China Building (1950), guarded by two fierce stone lions. Between it and the sea is the cenotaph, memorial to the dead of two world wars and the 1989 Tiananmen Square massacre. On the other side is Chater Garden, once home to the Hong Kong Cricket Club.

Statue of Sir Thomas Jackson, architect

HONG KONG PARK

In a space-deprived concrete jungle such as Hong Kong, this modern little park is a joy to wander in. Visit it after a morning's shopping to refresh yourself, but don't expect rose borders or ancient trees – it is a series of scenes artificially created with plants and concrete structures.

Artificial paradise Hong Kong Park, opened in 1991, is a small miracle of artificiality. Its architects used what little original landscape existed and built the park into the contours of the hillside. It is fun to walk through the aviary, where tree-high walkways take you cheek by bill with fascinating and brilliantly plumaged tropical birds.

The conservatory, the biggest one in the world, contains biospheres maintaining arid, humid and just plain flashy plant environments. The utterly artificial waterfalls are beautifully designed and give a refreshing look and sound. Everywhere the local, indigenous plants are grown. In particular, the enormous variety of bamboos – from tiny, delicate-stemmed varieties to the huge ones used in scaffolding – are on display, all labelled for your edification.

Refreshments old and new The Museum of Teaware in Flagstaff House, the oldest building in Hong Kong, deserves an afternoon all to itself. Flagstaff House is a charming and elegant piece of mid-19th-century architecture, and the exhibition of teapots and the like will bring out the collector in almost anyone. After visiting it, you might like to hit the happy hour (4–7) in the park's bar and restaurant. Most afternoons the park is full of elegantly dressed parties posing for wedding photos, having just emerged from the register office that is in the park grounds.

HIGHLIGHTS

- Walk-in aviary
- Artificial waterfalls
- Conservatory
- Flagstaff House and Museum of Teaware
- Observation tower
- *Bonsai* trees in T'ai Chi Garden

INFORMATION

- ✚ E8
- ✉ Main entrance: Supreme Court Road, Central. Nearest entrance for Museum of Teaware: Cotton Tree Drive, Central
- ☎ Museum: 28869 0690
- 🕐 Park: daily 7AM–11PM. Museum: Thu–Tue 10–5. Closed Wed, 24–25 Dec, 1 Jan and first three days of Chinese New Year
- 🍴 Café/bar in park (£)
- Ⓔ Admiralty
- 🚌 Buses 12, 23B, 33, 40, 103; get off at first stop in Cotton Tree Drive
- ♿ Good
- ⊡ Free
- ↔ Botanical & Zoological Gardens (➤ 32)

15

STAR FERRY

Riding the Star Ferry, between Kowloon and Hong Kong Island, has to be one of the most spectacular ferry trips in the world. For just HK$1.70 you get a panoramic view of the harbour as you duck and dive around massive dredgers, speeding launches, and all the rag-tag and bobtail vessels that skitter about these waters.

HIGHLIGHTS

- Shops in Tsim Sha Tsui ferry terminal
- Land reclamation projects, particularly beside Wan Chai
- Vista to east and west along shipping lane
- Hong Kong & Shanghai Banking Corporation building
- Bank of China Tower
- Convention and Exhibition Centre
- Views of Peak and Mid Levels
- Early evening jostling of cruise boats at Queen's Pier

INFORMATION

- E8/F7/F8
- Salisbury Road, Tsim Sha Tsui (Kowloon); Edinburgh Place, Central (Hong Kong Island); Sea Front Road, Wan Chai (Hong Kong Island)
- Hotline: 2366 2576
- Daily 6:30AM–11:30PM
- Small café before Central ferry terminal gate (£)
- Tsim Sha Tsui; Central; Wan Chai
- Main buses leave from bus stations at the three terminals
- Lower decks more accessible
- Cheap
- Central: Exchange Square (► 34), Statue Square (► 36). Tsim Sha Tsui: Space Museum (► 42), Museum of Art (► 43)

Looking back Journey time on the Star Ferry, which has been operating since 1898, is less than ten minutes on a good day, but the views of the cityscape on both sides of the harbour are excellent. The terminal on the Tsim Sha Tsui side sits beside the incongruous Hong Kong Cultural Centre (1989), with its smooth-tiled surface and lack of windows (► 51). As the ferry sets off on its journey to Hong Kong Island, you can see the long pink and black striped outlines of the Hong Kong Museum of Art (► 43).

Looking forwards Ahead of you, on the Island itself, the stunning architecture of the reclaimed shoreline opens up, dominated by the Convention and Exhibition Centre, with its twin towers of the New World Harbour View and Hyatt hotels. Behind it is Central Plaza, the tallest office building in Hong Kong at 78 storeys (► 50). West of these buildings are the General Post Office and the striped towers of the Stock Exchange, built by Remo Riva (1986). Behind these are the Hong Kong & Shanghai Banking Corporation building (► 51), all glass and innards, and the 74-storey angular Bank of China Tower, with its apparently bad *feng shui* (► 50). Try to pinpoint the various tower blocks, each one competing with the others for advertising space, harbour views and a position in the *Guinness Book of Records*.

MUSEUM OF HISTORY

This little gem of a Hong Kong history museum, both user-friendly and informative, is a good place to spend an hour or so, especially given its location in one of Hong Kong's relatively quiet spots – Kowloon Park.

Exhibits The museum does an excellent job of turning what might be a dry set of historical records into an understandable account of the lives of the people who have inhabited Hong Kong over the years. There is a model sampan to peer into, the interior of a modest Hakka home, and some of the costumes of the various peoples who migrated south from China into the New Territories. Coming into more recent times, there is a full-scale replica of a street in the city of Victoria, as Central was once known. The exhibits are fascinating, especially the entire medicine shop that was shifted lock, stock and barrel from its demolition site in Wan Chai. Other façades in the 19th-century street include a pawnshop, opium den, print shop, tea-house and a shop selling dried fish. Later exhibits show the burgeoning Hong Kong manufacturing industry of the 1950s that produced cheap enamelware and tin toys.

The photographic collection Even more telling are the photographs in the museum; some are of the plague that hit Hong Kong in the late 19th century, others show daily life in the streets of Hong Kong, and several much later photographs illustrate the effects the worst typhoons and landslides have had on the territory.

HIGHLIGHTS

- Early photographs
- Full-size replica of sampan
- Herbalist shop
- Interior of Eurasian family home
- *Chai mun* (ornamental plank) from temple
- Kowloon Park

INFORMATION

- F6
- Kowloon Park (near Haiphong Road entrance), Tsim Sha Tsui
- 2367 1124
- Mon–Thu, Sat 10–6; Sun and holidays 1–6. Closed Fri and some holidays
- Tsim Sha Tsui
- Excellent
- Cheap
- Space Museum (➤ 42) Museum of Art (➤ 43)
- Audio-visual shows

Queen's Road c.1915

17

OCEAN PARK

HIGHLIGHTS

- Atoll reef aquarium
- Shark aquarium
- Butterfly house
- Middle Kingdom
- Ocean Theatre animal shows
- Raging River flume ride
- Aviary
- Bird shows at bird theatre
- Dragon Ride

INFORMATION

- ✚ Off map to south
- ⊠ Aberdeen, Hong Kong
- ☎ 2837 8888 or 2555 3554
- ◑ Daily 10–6
- 🍽 Several fast-food eateries inside (£)
- 🚌 Ocean Park Citibus leaves from Exchange Square Bus Terminus every half-hour
- ♿ Excellent
- 💷 Expensive
- ↔ Water World (➤ 58)
- ❓ Height restrictions on some rides

Dolphin ride

Wildlife, history, scenic views, arts and crafts, animal shows – quite apart from spectacular rides – make up a whole, frenetic day's entertainment.

There is so much on offer here, the first thing to do on arrival is to find out the times and locations of the animal show; plan the rest of your day around them. The rides really are stomach-turning, the creatures in the aquarium scary, and the animal and plant exhibits well-displayed and maintained. Don't miss the Raging River flume ride with the most breathtaking – literally – part at the end of the ride.

Most fun of all, perhaps, is the cable-car ride into the place. You dangle in a fragile little car, stopping and starting for no apparent reason as the wind whistles around and beneath you, with the sea gently boiling below. And to come out of the park you take a four-section, 227m-long escalator ride.

Try to avoid the weekends, when the place gets very crowded, and note there are minimum height restrictions on some rides.

TEMPLE STREET

This street really comes alive at about 7PM each night, when stalls are set up along either side and are hung with outrageous T-shirts, lingerie, jeans, and other consumer goodies. Earlier in the day stalls do a brisk trade in jade.

After dark The market is full of bargains such as silk shirts, leather items and bric-à-brac, as well as jeans and T-shirts. Nothing on sale is very 'ethnic' as this is really a locals' market rather than a tourist one. After about 7:30PM the street is blocked off to traffic, and at the crossroads right in the middle of the market two fresh-fish restaurants set up their tables. Their counters, also out in the street, contain all manner of wriggling things that you can pick out to be cooked for your dinner.

Jade market At the end of the street and to the left is the jade market, which starts to close up at about 3PM. Hundreds of stalls here sell all kinds of jade, ranging in colour from white through green to purple. Locals spend the afternoon bargaining over prices, which range from cheap to a king's ransom – unless you know what you are doing this is not the place to make a major investment.

In adjoining streets are vegetable and fruit stalls, shops selling fabrics and traditional red-embroidered Chinese wedding outfits, and many Chinese medicine shops. If you are lucky, you may catch a Chinese opera performance, sung in Cantonese on a makeshift stage of bamboo and canvas.

As you walk along, listen out for the clacking sound of a traditional game of mahjong being played in the flats above the market.

HIGHLIGHTS

- Fresh fish set out on stalls
- Fortune-tellers
- Chinese medicine shops
- Shops selling traditional Chinese wedding clothes
- Jade market
- Yau Ma Tei Typhoon Shelter, to the west
- Racks of T-shirts
- Exotic vegetables in vegetable market

INFORMATION

- F5–6
- Temple Street, Kansu Street, Reclamation Street, Kowloon
- Jade market: 10–4. Temple Street market: 8AM–11PM. Vegetable market: early morning and early evening
- Seafood restaurants and hawker centre in Temple Street (£)
- Jordan
- Good
- Free
- Lei Cheng Uk Museum (➤ 35)

41

SPACE MUSEUM

HIGHLIGHTS

- Omnimax Theatre
- Moon rocks
- *Mercury* space capsule
- Hall of Space Science
- Solar telescope
- Planetarium show
- Hall of Astronomy

INFORMATION

- ✚ F7
- ✉ Hong Kong Cultural Centre, Tsim Sha Tsui, Kowloon
- ☎ 3734 2722
- ⏰ Mon, Wed–Fri 1–9; Sat, Sun, some holidays 10–9. Closed Tue and some holidays
- 🚇 Tsim Sha Tsui
- 🚌 Tsim Sha Tsui bus station
- ⛴ Star Ferry to Central and Wan Chai
- ♿ Excellent
- 🖐 Moderate
- ✛ Hong Kong Science Museum (► 58)
- ❓ No children under three in the Omnimax Theatre

This museum, which has one of the largest and most advanced planetariums in the world, is fascinating for kids of all ages, with plenty of hands-on exhibits, a genuine **Mercury** *space capsule, and daily Omnimax and Space Theatre shows.*

Layout and Omnimax The museum's pink, oval building is in itself stunning, and there is much to lure the visitor inside. There are three exhibitions: the Hall of Astronomy, the Hall of Space Science and, the most popular, the Omnimax Theatre and Planetarium. If you haven't seen an Omnimax movie before, then seize the chance here. The audience sits back in tilted seats and gazes ahead and up at a screen that covers most of the ceiling and front wall. If you get at all queasy on fun-fair rides then don't watch the parts where someone jumps out of an aeroplane or travels around in a roller-coaster as these seem very real.

Exhibition Halls The Space Science Exhibition includes bits of moon rock, the actual *Mercury* space capsule piloted by Scott Carpenter in 1962 and plenty more to thrill space enthusiasts. In the Museum of Astronomy is a solar telescope through which visitors can look at the sun. Did you know that ancient Chinese astronomers were the first to spot Halley's Comet, the first to use gunpowder and the first to chart the movements of the stars?

Gravity chair, with astronaut in action shown behind

MUSEUM OF ART

Here is a beautifully laid-out series of galleries containing displays of Chinese painting and calligraphy, both ancient and modern, many stunning ancient artefacts, and a collection of jade, ivory and pottery.

Chinese antiquities Opened in 1989 along with the other parts of the Hong Kong Cultural Centre complex, the museum has six galleries, four containing Chinese antiquities, local artists' work, and pictures of historical note as well as artistic worth. The Chinese antiquities section has thousands of exhibits, from rhino-horn cups to burial goods and tomb adornments. Of particular interest are two large Tang Dynasty (AD 618–906) tomb guardians in the form of mythical beasts. The jade and ivory carvings in the Decorative Arts gallery are especially lovely.

Art galleries The best gallery is the one containing old pictures and prints of Hong Kong. It is hard to believe that the sandy beaches and jungle-filled hills could have become such a different kind of jungle in so short a space of time. The painting of the city of Victoria (as the built-up part of Hong Kong was called) is a revelation of just how far the colony has come since the early 19th century.

The works in the contemporary art gallery are divided into decades, and it is particularly interesting to see the development of local art since the 1950s. There is also a collection of calligraphy and Chinese paintings, and a special gallery for international exhibitions. Between galleries, leather armchairs facing the enormous corridor windows allow you to enjoy the wonderful vista.

HIGHLIGHTS

- Han Dynasty pottery watch-tower
- Tang Dynasty tomb guardians
- Translucent rhino-horn cups
- Description of Quing kiln
- Painting of city of Victoria (1854)
- Painting of Wyndham Street
- *The Baptism* in contemporary art gallery
- Models of merchant boats and sea-going junk
- Model of Guangzhou
- Lithograph of Hong Kong Harbour

INFORMATION

- F7
- Hong Kong Cultural Centre, Tsim Sha Tsui
- 2734 2167
- Mon–Wed, Fri, Sat 10–6; Sun 1–6. Closed Thu and some public holidays
- Café within Cultural Centre complex (£)
- Tsim Sha Tsui
- Tsim Sha Tsui bus station
- Star Ferry to Wan Chai and Central
- Excellent
- Inexpensive
- Star Ferry (➤ 38)

PAK TAI TEMPLE

HIGHLIGHTS

- Roof decorations
- Statue of Pak Tai
- Burial offerings
- Nearby Hung Sheng Temple (Queen's Road East) and Tai Wong Street bird market
- Nearby Wan Chai Post Office (Queen's Road East; opened 1915)

INFORMATION

- ✚ F9
- ✉ Lung On Street, off Queen's Road East, Wan Chai
- 🚇 Wan Chai
- 🚌 Bus 260 or 15 from Central; get off at Wan Chai Market
- ♿ None
- 🎫 Free, but donations welcome
- ↔ Hong Kong Park, Flagstaff House and Museum of Teaware (➤ 37)
  Tai Wong Temple (➤ 55)

Of the many temples in the area, be sure to visit this elderly one, for in its back halls you can see craftsmen working at one of the most unusual trades you may ever come across – the making of the modern paper equivalents of prehistoric grave goods.

Pak Tai Built in the 1860s, this temple is dedicated to Pak Tai, the military protector whose job is to maintain peace rather than bring good luck in battle. His representation in this temple is a 17th-century copper statue seated on a throne. The statue has a blackened face, real hair and is dressed in sumptuously embroidered clothes. Around it are ranged four figures that represent warriors and scholars.

Like all Taoist temples, this one has no set service times. People come, at any time, to pray or make an offering, or to seek help regarding their future using the bamboo sticks called *chim*. The air is full of the heady mixture of incense and the perfume from fruit and flowers left by worshippers.

Model business Be sure to visit the side room of the temple where men sit making models of everything the recently deceased might need in the afterlife. Rolls Royces, servants, houses, suites of furniture, VCRs and money are all painstakingly made out of paper and thin strips of bamboo. The models are collected together and displayed at the funeral as an indication of the person's prestige and then burnt so that they can accompany the deceased on his or her journey to heaven. It is lucky for archaeologists that prehistoric peoples did not use paper for the goods they despatched with their dead.

TEN THOUSAND BUDDHAS TEMPLE

A half-hour train ride out of Hong Kong brings you to this fairytale temple set on a hillside overlooking the estates and towers of the satellite town of Sha Tin.

Bountiful Buddhas To reach the temple you must first climb 431 steps through the open hillside. Known locally as Man Fat Sze Temple, this is a Buddhist shrine which has, since it was built in the 1950s, become the Ten Thousand Buddhas Temple thanks to the donations of small statues by grateful worshippers over the years. The statues are all different – either black or covered in gold leaf – and in each one Buddha strikes a different pose that represents the different stages on his road to enlightenment.

Panoramas and pagodas From the edge of the courtyard there are magnificent views over Sha Tin. The courtyard houses a tiered pagoda and the statues of some of Buddha's followers. Higher up again is another set of four temples, one containing Hong Kong's second-tallest Buddha statue, and another the embalmed, gilded remains of Yuet Kai, the monk who founded the monastery.

HIGHLIGHTS

- Thousands of small statues of Buddha
- Tallest standing Buddha statue in Hong Kong
- Embalmed and gilded body of monastery's founder
- Statues of Buddha's followers
- Views over Sha Tin
- 400-odd steps up to monastery
- Views of Amah Rock

INFORMATION

- ✚ Off map to north
- ✉ Close to Pai Tau Street, Sha Tin, New Territories
- 🕐 Daily 8–6. Particularly busy around Chinese New Year. In 1997 the temple was temporarily closed after a landslide. Check with HKTA before visiting (➤ 88–9)
- 🚇 Sha Tin
- ♿ None
- 💰 Free, but donations welcome

Courtyard of the Ten Thousand Buddhas Temple

45

23

WONG TAI SIN TEMPLE

HIGHLIGHTS

- Main altar including painting of Wong Tai Sin
- Garden of Nine Dragon Wall
- Fortune-telling arcade
- Clinic Block
- Stalls outside selling windmills and hell money
- Chinese gardens at rear of complex
- Side altar in main temple dedicated to monkey god
- Incinerators for burning offerings

INFORMATION

- H1
- Wong Tai Sin Estate; follow signs from MTR station
- Information hotline: 2801 1777 or 2327 8141
- Daily 7–5. Main temple is not always accessible
- Wong Tai Sin
- Good
- Free, but donations welcome

If temples were businesses, then Wong Tai Sin Temple would be a hypermarket. Don't go during Chinese New Year unless you are willing to risk having your hair set on fire by hundreds of devotees waving joss-sticks as they whirl from one deity to the next.

Wong Tai Sin This large Taoist temple, built in 1973 in Chinese style and situated amongst high-rise residential blocks, is dedicated to Wong Tai Sin, an ex-shepherd who was taught how to cure all ills by a passing deity. In modern-day Hong Kong, Wong Tai Sin is a very popular god, as he is in charge of the fortunes of gamblers. He can also be sought out by those who are ill or worried about their health, or by people asking for help in business matters.

Temple interior The stadium-sized temple complex is huge, from the main temple where Wong Tai Sin is represented by a painting rather than a statue, to the turtle-ponds, libraries, medicine halls and what is almost a small shopping centre of fortune-tellers. The temple is built to represent the five geomantic elements of gold, wood, water, fire and earth. In the Yue Heung Shrine are fire and earth; gold is represented in the Bronze Luen Pavilion where the portrait of Wong Tai Sin is kept; and the Library Hall and water fountain represent wood and water respectively.

The Temple also caters for those who venerate Confucius, represented in the Confucius Hall, while Buddhists come here to worship the Buddhist goddess of mercy, Kuan Yin, in the Three Saints Hall alongside Kwan Ti and the eight immortals.

TIGER BALM GARDENS

There is something nostalgic about this rather sad, crumbling place. The paint is faded, the concrete is cracked and the statues have been removed or have merged into their surroundings. But as a monument to the transience of wealth and power, this place is second to none.

Visions of hell Tiger Balm Gardens (Aw Boon Haw Gardens) were built in 1935 by the millionaire philanthropist Aw Boon Haw, who made his fortune from Tiger Balm ointment, still rubbed into sore joints throughout Hong Kong and South-East Asia. The garden is full of concrete statues of figures in Chinese mythology and depicts victims being tortured in hell, although the concrete sea lions stuck for ever in a concrete sea are perhaps more worthy of pity. At the very back of the garden is a bas-relief concrete panel showing the horrors that befall those who maltreat their elders, forcibly adopt children, commit adultery or generally behave badly. The ninth degree of hell looks the worst, although what the goat is doing is a mystery, while in the eighth level, sinners are run over by a 1940s truck!

Other sights The gardens have a pagoda (said to have cost HK\$1 million in 1930); the view from the top is very good. There are also little grottoes, caves with Chinese myths depicted inside, and a model of the jade bridge over which the righteous walk to their next incarnation. The gardens are surrounded by towering apartment blocks that make you wonder if some of the indignities of hell aren't already with us.

HIGHLIGHTS

- The villa
- Phoenix, dragon and lion in frieze behind villa
- Mazes of steps and grottoes
- Statues of Buddha explaining stages of enlightenment
- Ten Courts of Hell
- Truck in eighth level of Hell
- Jade bridge through which good people are reincarnated into a rich family
- Cactus plants near waterfall

INFORMATION

- H9
- Tai Hang Road, Happy Valley
- Daily 9:30–4
- Causeway Bay
- Bus 11 from Central Bus Terminal
- None
- Free

Tiger Balm Gardens

25

STANLEY

HIGHLIGHTS

- Views from bus to Stanley
- Tin Hau Temple
- Stanley Beach
- St Stephen's Beach
- Stanley Military Cemetery
- Stanley market
- Kuan Yin Temple

INFORMATION

- ✚ Off map to south
- 🕐 Market: 10:30–9.
  Temple: 6–6
- 🍴 Restaurants (££–£££) and
  pub food (£) in Stanley
  Main Street. Avoid
  expensive café in market
- 🚍 Bus 6 or 260 from Central
  Bus Terminus
- ♿ Excellent
- ❓ Tours (➤ 19)

The most stunning thing about a trip to the town of Stanley, in the south of Hong Kong Island, is the scenic, and at times precarious, journey there. Get an upstairs seat on the double-decker bus – the ride is as good as any at Ocean Park.

Temples Most visitors come to Stanley Village for its market, but it has many other attractions. Close to the market is the Tin Hau Temple, first built on this spot in the early 1700s. The bell and drum are said to have belonged to a famous pirate, Cheung Po-Tsai. The bell was cast in 1767, and it is thought that the pirate used it to send messages to his ships. The temple also contains the skin of a tiger, shot in Stanley in 1942. During the Japanese invasion the villagers took refuge inside the temple, and although the building was hit twice, neither bomb exploded. Further along the road is a second temple, dedicated to Kuan Yin, the goddess of mercy. Claims have been made that the 6m statue of the goddess has moved. Nowadays Stanley is a commuter town, popular with expatriate workers.

Beaches and the market The beach at Stanley is a good one, and a short bus ride further along takes you to St Stephen's Beach where there is a graveyard for all the soldiers who have died in Hong Kong since Britain first claimed the colony. Stanley's famous market is quite good, although it is now rather touristy. It has several linen shops as well as stalls selling clothes made in other Asian countries.

Stanley market

HONG KONG's
best

ARCHITECTURE

Bank of China Tower

**See Top 25 Sights for
EXCHANGE SQUARE ➤ 34**

Geomancers

Almost all building that goes on in Hong Kong is overseen by a *feng shui* (literally 'wind and water') master, someone who knows how the life force, or *chi*, moves around the planet's surface. Sharp angles send out bad *chi*, while strategically placed water and mirrors can enhance good *chi* by allowing it to flow smoothly and not get trapped in corners. The master may have much to say about the building's structure, he studies the site and will decide on auspicious day for starting work.

BANK OF CHINA TOWER

Designed by the Chinese-American architect, I M Pei and built between 1985 and 1990, this 300m-high, 70-storey tower dominates the Hong Kong skyline. The building soars upwards in a series of triangles towards a prism at the top. Amazingly, it is built with no internal supporting columns. The entrance hall has barrelled vaults in the style of a Ming Dynasty tomb – a typically Hong Kong mixture of the ultra-modern and the historic.

✚ E8 ✉ No 1 Garden Road, Central 🕐 Weekdays 9–5 🚇 Central 💲 Free

CENTRAL PLAZA

Completed in 1992, Central Plaza is Hong Kong's tallest building at 78 storeys and 374m (counting the spire). The tower is triangular, giving it two views of the harbour. Majestic both inside and out, it incorporates a huge public space, in the form of a piazza at ground level and a through-walkway on the first level. The whole mood is one of brooding neo-classical grandeur, with a vast lobby containing two-storey palm trees and some terrific artwork. The architects were Dennis Lau and Ng Chun Man.

✚ F8 ✉ Harbour Road, Wan Chai 🚇 Wan Chai 💲 Free

HONG KONG & SHANGHAI BANKING CORPORATION BUILDING

This 1985 building, designed by Norman Foster and prefabricated in several different continents at a cost of over US$1 billion, looks as if it's been turned inside out. The supporting structures appear on the outside, all mechanical parts are exposed and many walls are glass. A geomancer decided the alignment and angles of the escalators.

➕ E8   ✉ Des Voeux Road and Statue Square, Central   🚇 Central
🎫 Free

HONG KONG CONVENTION & EXHIBITION CENTRE

Built on reclaimed land, this massive complex looks bland when approached from the harbour, despite the fact that its towers contain two of the island's most prestigious hotels – the New World Harbour View and the Grand Hyatt – plus some 1,800sq m of exhibition space. On the harbour side of the exhibition hall is a seven-storey plate-glass window. Escalators go alongside it up to the seventh floor, giving great harbour views. The ninth storey has a recreation centre used by residents of the apartments in the complex.

➕ F8   ✉ 1 Convention Avenue, Wan Chai   ☎ 2582 8888
🚇 Wan Chai   🎫 Free

HONG KONG CULTURAL CENTRE

Designed by the government's architectural services department and built in 1989, this is one of Hong Kong's most controversial buildings. It has a huge sloping roof that is matched by the dome of the nearby Space Museum, and is uniformly pink. The building is also windowless – rather odd as it would have one of the most dynamic views in the world. Inside, everything is very modern, especially the sparse auditoria with their apparently unsupported balconies. At the rear is a harbourfront walkway.

➕ F7   ✉ Salisbury Road, Tsim Sha Tsui
☎ 2734 20109   🚇 Tsim Sha Tsui
🎫 Free

THE WHAMPOA

The Whampoa may not have the statistics of other buildings here, but it must be one of the few ship-shaped concrete developments in the world! Built by Robert Lam into the space once occupied by a dry dock, it is a shopping centre – with cinemas and ice rink – that looks as if it is about to set sail.

➕ G5   ✉ Sung King Street, Hung Hom   🚌 Bus 6 from Hanlow Road or taxi from Tsim Sha Tsui MTR   🎫 Free

Feng shui in practice

When the Conrad Hotel was redesigned recently, coins were buried beneath the floor of the downstairs lobby, itself in the shape of a Chinese coin. The carp and lily paintings on the walls of the hotel lobby represent pools of water, so bringing in good *chi* and holding it there. The Chinese restaurant in the Excelsior Hotel was designed with temporary moving partitions so that the series of small rooms could periodically be opened up into a large loop, thus allowing a good flow of *chi* through the restaurant.

Hong Kong Convention and Exhibition Centre

GREEN SPACES

See Top 25 Sights for
HONG KONG PARK ► 37
VICTORIA PEAK ► 27

CHEUNG CHAU ISLAND

Cheung Chau has two good beaches, lots of seafood restaurants, some interesting temples, caves, an annual bun festival, windsurfing equipment and bicycles for hire, good walks and no traffic.

Cheung Chau Island

🕐 Hourly ferries start around 6:30ᴀᴍ. Last ferry returns around 11:30ᴘᴍ 🚢 Outlying Islands Pier, Central 🎫 Moderate

KOWLOON PARK
► 59

LAMMA ISLAND

Great beaches, no cars, plenty of good seafood restaurants and places to walk. Also a power station and a huge quarry, but these do not spoil a great day out. Nicest beach is at Mo Tat Wan.

🕐 Ferries run approx 7ᴀᴍ–10:30ᴘᴍ 🚢 Outlying Islands Pier, Central 🎫 Moderate; double at weekends

PENG CHAU

This tiny island is quite densely populated, with a crowded village, a market, and some cottage industries. Sewage can make swimming on the east side of the island unpleasant.

🕐 Ferries start around 7ᴀᴍ and run hourly. Last ferry returns around 11:30ᴘᴍ 🍴 Cafés 🚢 Outlying Islands Pier, Central 🎫 Moderate; double at weekends

Country parks

Hong Kong Island has five country parks, areas of protected countryside, all linked together along the 50km Hong Kong Trail, a well-laid out footpath. Each park has barbecue sites and other facilities, but they do get very crowded at weekends. However, if you venture any distance along the trail you soon leave the crowds behind. The most accessible park is probably Pok Fu Lam Country Park, which can be reached on foot from the Peak or by the No. 15 bus from Central.

TAI TAM COUNTRY PARK

An excellent country park, perfect for when the crowds begin to oppress you. You can walk along the coast and around a reservoir, past World War II bunkers and pill boxes. Bring strong shoes and something to drink if you intend to walk for long.

➕ I/KR/9/10 🚇 Wan Chai MTR, then minibus 16M or 🚌 Bus 6 from Exchange Square to Hong Kong Cricket Club, then walk past petrol station and take first left up steps

VICTORIA PARK

This relatively enormous patch of green is used to the full. There are sports pitches, a pool and some pleasant green walks. Early morning *t'ai chi ch'uan* takes place and many events are staged here.

➕ G8–H8 ✉ Causeway Bay, Hong Kong Island 🚋 Tram from Wan Chai or Central (look for one labelled 'Causeway Bay') 🎫 Free

TEMPLES

Other places of worship

Many religions are practised in Hong Kong beside Taoism and Buddhism. The colony has a synagogue and two mosques as well as many churches. The two most prominent churches are the Roman Catholic cathedral, built in 1880 by Portuguese Catholics from Macau, and the Anglican St John's Cathedral in Garden Road, built in 1847. Both are open to the public and well worth a visit, if only for the sense they give of what life must have been like in 19th-century Hong Kong.

LU PAN TEMPLE

Usually empty and quiet, this is the only temple in Hong Kong dedicated to Lu Pan, the master builder who repaired the pillars of heaven. His festival is celebrated by construction workers. The temple has elaborate roof ceramics and carvings above the door.

➕ B8   ✉ Li Po Lung Path, off Belcher's Street, Kennedy Town
⏰ Daily 8–7   🚌 Bus 3 from Rumsey Steet, Central   💷 Free

MAN MO TEMPLE, TAI PO ➤ 19

HUNG SHENG TEMPLE

This temple is dedicated to the scholar Hung Sheng, who was able to foretell the weather. It is built quite a way back into the rock-face behind it and supports several elderly fortune-tellers who have set up little shrines around it.

➕ F9   ✉ 131 Queen's Road East, Wan Chai   ⏰ Daily 8–6
🚇 Wan Chai   💷 Free

TIN HAU TEMPLE, CAUSEWAY BAY

Dedicated to Tin Hau, the goddess who protects seafarers, this is one of the many temples that were once scattered around Hong Kong's coastline. The temple is about 200 years old, although it has been renovated, and is perched on a rock above the road.

➕ H8   ✉ Tin Hau Street, Causeway Bay   ⏰ Daily 8–6   🚇 Tin Hau
💷 Free

TIN HAU TEMPLE, KOWLOON

Kowloon's temple of the goddess of the sea and seafarers, after which Temple Street is named, is one of Kowloon's oldest and once looked over the sea, now several blocks away.

➕ F5   ✉ Market Street, Kowloon   ⏰ Daily 8–6   🚇 Jordan
💷 Free

TIN HAU TEMPLE, REPULSE BAY

Yet another Tin Hau temple dedicated to the goddess of fisherfolk. This one has a longevity bridge in front of it; crossing it is said to add three years to your life.

✉ Repulse Bay Beach   ⏰ Daily 8–6   🚌 Bus 6 or
61 from Central Bus Terminus   💷 Free

Roof decoration of Wong Tai Sin Temple

MARKETS

Bird markets

Songbirds have always played an important part in Hong Kong's social life. Keeping the birds is a male activity, and a man taking his bird for a walk is a common sight in parks. There are regular impromptu bird-song competitions, when a judge listens to the songs of birds in different cages and large sums of money are wagered on which bird will win the prize. The bird-cages are little works of art in themselves, often carved out of mahogany or bamboo.

See Top 25 Sights for
JADE MARKET ► 41
STANLEY MARKET ► 48
TEMPLE STREET NIGHT MARKET ► 41

APLIU STREET

Tour buses rarely include this area in their itineraries, but it is a thoroughly Chinese market selling clothes, cheap CDs and sundry items. The Golden Shopping Centre (► 73) is in the vicinity.

➕ E3 ✉ Apliu Street, Sham Shui Po, Kowloon ⏰ Daily mid-morning–late 🚇 Sham Shui Po

BIRD MARKET

This market is dedicated to the sale of songbirds and all the associated paraphernalia from bird-seed to the often elaborate cages. The local bird-fanciers prefer the tiny birds, but the market also sells more exotic creatures such as parrots and mynahs. Look for cages of crickets, which are fed to the birds with chopsticks.

➕ F3 ✉ Yuen Po Street, Mong Kok ⏰ Daily 7AM–8PM 🚇 Mong Kok

Bird market

FA YUEN STREET

Two blocks, heaving with local colour and some amazing bargains in clothes.

➕ F3 ✉ Prince Edward MTR ⏰ Daily 10AM–late

FLOWER MARKET

A whole street is given over to cut-flower and potted-plant stalls. Interesting plants to look for here are the carnivorous pitcher plants and the beautiful but very expensive *bonsai*. Silk flowers are also sold.

➕ F3 ✉ Flower Market Road, Kowloon ⏰ Daily 9–6 🚇 Prince Edward

JARDINE'S BAZAAR

This is one of Hong Kong's oldest street markets, full of excellent bargains in clothes, with interesting food stores and shops selling clothes and handbags.

➕ G8 ✉ Jardine's Bazaar and Jardine's Crescent, Causeway Bay ⏰ Daily mid-morning–late 🚇 Causeway Bay

Card players near Jade Market

LADIES' MARKET

This market easily rivals Temple Street, and although once dedicated to ladies' clothes only, it now has bargains for everyone, especially printed T-shirts, belts, cheap jeans and watches. It covers about four blocks of densest Mong Kok, so you have to love crowds to shop here.

➕ F4 ✉ Tung Choi Street, Mong Kok ⏰ Daily noon–10 🚇 Mong Kok

LI YUEN STREET EAST AND WEST

A clothes, handbag, fabric and accessories market, one of Hong Kong's oldest, with some excellent bargains, particularly in leather goods. It could be combined with the factory outlets in the Pedder Building (➤ 77).

➕ D8 ✉ Off Queen's Road Central, Central ⏰ Daily noon–late 🚇 Central

MARBLE ROAD MARKET

This is a busy working local market with fresh produce, a nearby fresh-fish market and some bargains in T-shirts and clothes.

➕ J7 ✉ Marble Road, North Point ⏰ Daily noon–late 🚋 Tram from Causeway Bay, Wan Chai or Central

UPPER LASCAR ROW

A flea market set alongside more up-market shops and selling the same kind of bric-à-brac, records, curios and the occasional antique.

➕ D8 ✉ Off Queen's Road West, Sheung Wan ⏰ Daily 11–6 🚇 Sheung Wan

WESTERN MARKET

Gift items, crafts, paintings, fabrics and restaurants.

➕ D7 ✉ New Market Street, Sheung Wan ⏰ Daily 10–7 🚇 Sheung Wan

Flower markets

There are several markets dedicated to flowers in Hong Kong, selling mostly cut flowers or silk ones. Around Chinese New Year, flower markets spring up all around – a particularly big one is held in Victoria Park. Families go there to buy kumquat trees, orange trees and plum-blossom branches to decorate their houses. Flowers particularly favoured at this time are exquisitely perfumed narcissi and gladioli.

SHOPPING CENTRES

Pacific Place

Pacific Place forms part of a vast underground-linked chain of shopping malls that spreads out around Admiralty MTR station. Built around a very tall atrium, decorated in granite pink, chrome and glass, it is visually captivating as well as a great place to shop. It consists mostly of clothes shops, with three hotels, restaurants, fast-food joints, a huge branch of Marks & Spencer, a supermarket, three cinemas and a Seibu Japanese department store all thrown in. The main concourse is often the venue for free concerts.

Shopping in Admiralty Building

CITY PLAZA I AND II

This centre is used by lots of locals and is rarely visited by tourists. It has shops with fixed prices and its two skating rinks – roller and ice – have attracted childrenswear shops and toyshops. There are also men's and women's clothes shops.

K8 ✉ 1111 King's Road, Taikoo Shing 🕘 Daily 9–8 🚇 Tai Koo

THE LANDMARK

A very exclusive mall with all the big-name designer labels and prices to match. There are numerous cafés and a huge atrium with an impressive fountain where free concerts are frequently given. Another attraction is the musical clock, ornamented with figures from the Chinese zodiac.

D8 ✉ Des Voeux Road and Pedder Street, Central 🕘 Daily 9–8 🚇 Central

NEW WORLD CENTRE

Slightly more up-market and rarefied than the other malls, but a bit gloomy, the New World Centre has lots of shops selling silks and jade, and some excellent rosewood and lacquer furniture shops. It also has a reasonably priced Japanese Seiyu department store. Not a place to sit back and admire the architecture.

F7 ✉ Salisbury Road, Tsim Sha Tsui 🕘 Daily 9–8 🚇 Tsim Sha Tsui

OCEAN TERMINAL

This megamall stretches along the length of Canton Road and seems to go on for ever. It has a wide variety of shops ranging from the usual U2, G2000, Giordano and Bossini to interesting furniture and fabric shops.

F6 ✉ Canton Road, Tsim Sha Tsui 🕘 Daily 9–8 🚇 Tsim Sha Tsui

PACIFIC PLACE

You could live and die in this shopping centre without ever having to leave it. See panel, left.

E8 ✉ 88 Queensway, Central 🕘 Daily 9–8 🚇 Admiralty

PINOY WORLD

This shopping centre is dedicated to all things Filipino, including shops, restaurants and live-music performances. Hong Kong has about 130,000 migrant

Filipino workers who all get the day off on Sunday and who tend to congregate around the open spaces of Central. This shopping complex is aimed at that market and offers a variety of products not easily found elsewhere, including delicacies and crafts from the Philippines as well as services such as shipping agents and employment agencies.

🔢 G4 ✉ Ma Tau Wai Road, Kowloon ⏰ Daily 9–8 🚍 Bus 5A from Tsim Sha Tsui Star Ferry

SHUN TAK CENTRE

The biggest mall in the western end of the island, this is built around a residential hotel, offices and the ferry terminal to Macau. It has large open spaces with cafés and food stalls, lots of local chain stores and some interesting clothes and leather shops. Worth popping into on a trip to Western Market for its air-conditioning and refreshments, as well as the shops.

🔢 D7 ✉ 200 Connaught Road, Sheung Wan ⏰ Daily 9–8 🚇 Sheung Wan

TIMES SQUARE

Another space-age supermall, this one having floors dedicated to certain products so that computer merchandise is on one floor, ladies' clothes are on another and so on. It is best avoided at weekends when vast crowds flood in. It is in the excellent shopping area of Causeway Bay with other plazas close by as well as several Japanese department stores and Chinese products stores, so if you have time to visit only one shopping area choose this one.

🔢 G8 ✉ Matheson Street, Causeway Bay ⏰ Daily 9–8 🚇 Causeway Bay

Pacific Place

Harbour City

The Harbour City complex in Tsim Sha Tsui is one of the world's longest shopping complexes and includes Ocean Centre, Ocean Galleries, a few hotels and Ocean Terminal. If you can't find what you want here, it probably doesn't exist.

STRICTLY FOR CHILDREN

**See Top 25 Sights for
OCEAN PARK ► 40**

More ideas

Like the rest of us, children enjoy spending money, and Hong Kong is a good place to blow that saved-up pocket money. Designer sportswear – fake and the real thing – can be found in the side streets of Mong Kok, Ocean Terminal has an enormous Toys'R'Us, and there are hundreds of shops around Nathan Road selling electronic toys and games. Very popular with boys of all ages are gas-powered, toy handguns (but make sure your own country allows them in).

CITY PLAZA II ICE PALACE AND ROLLERWORLD
This shopping centre houses two skating rinks – ice and roller. The admission price includes skate hire and two hours' skating. Located in the same building is Fourseas Bowling Centre.
K8   ✉ Tai Koo Shing, Hong Kong Island.   Cafés   Tai Koo Shing
Ice Palace: ☎ 2885 6697   Daily 7AM–10PM   Moderate
Rollerworld: ☎ 2567 0391   Daily 9–9   Moderate
Fourseas Bowling Centre: ☎ 2567 0763   Daily 9:30am–1AM
Moderate

DRAGON SHOPPING CENTRE
The main attraction of this shopping centre, opened in 1996, is the roller-coaster ride that whizzes about inside the building. There is also a skating rink and a video games centre. Get on with some serious shopping while the kids have fun.
E2   ✉ Yen Chow Street, Sham Shui Po   ☎ 2360 0982
Daily 11–10   Sham Shui Po MTR   Ride: inexpensive

HONG KONG SCIENCE MUSEUM
Excellent hands-on museum full of zany exhibits.
F6   ✉ Science Museum Road, Tsim Sha Tsui   ☎ 2732 3232
Tue–Fri 1–9; Sat–Sun 10–9. Closed Mon   Bus 6 from Hanlow Road or taxi from Tsim Sha Tsui MTR   Moderate

POK FU LAM PUBLIC RIDING SCHOOL
To the southwest of the Island, this riding school provides lessons for all abilities but is often fully booked, so phoning in advance is essential.
C10   ✉ 75 Reservoir Road, Pok Fu Lam
☎ 2551 0030   Sep–Jun. Closed Mon
Moderate

POLICE MUSEUM ► 59

REPULSE BAY
The pretty beach here gets very crowded on public holidays and at weekends, but there is a temple (► 53) and a modern shopping arcade to visit when the heat gets too much.
Bus 6, 61 from Central Bus Terminus   Free

WATER WORLD
A water park with chutes, slides, diving platforms and rides. Cheaper in the evening.
Off map to south   ✉ Ocean Park Road, Aberdeen   ☎ 2555 6055
Jul–Aug daily 9–9. Jun, Sep, Oct daily 10–6   Ocean Park Citibus from beside Central Bus Terminus   Moderate

Water World

FREE ATTRACTIONS

See Top 25 Sights for
BOTANICAL GARDENS ➤ 32
TIGER BALM GARDENS ➤ 47

CITY HALL COMPLEX
The City Hall complex has a garden where you can watch wedding parties posing for photos, plus several libraries containing rare material on microfilm, back copies of newspapers, and a wealth of material on local culture and issues. Bring your passport for ID.
✚ E8 ✉ Edinburgh Place, Central ☎ 9221 2840 🕐 Libraries: Mon–Thu 10–7; Fri 10–9; Sat 10–5; Sun 10–1 🚇 Central
🚢 Star Ferry

LAW UK FOLK MUSEUM
A genuine 200-year-old house furnished in Hakka style. Displays show how Hakka farmers lived.
✚ M10 ✉ 14 Kut Shing Street, Chai Wan ☎ 2896 7006
🕐 Tue–Sat 10–1, 2–6; Sun and holidays 1–6. Closed Mon and some holidays 🚇 Chai Wan

CHINESE UNIVERSITY OF HONG KONG ART GALLERY
This collection of Chinese art includes over 1,000 paintings and pieces of calligraphy, bronze seals from the Han Dynasty (AD 25–220), and over 400 jade flower carvings.
✚ Off map to north ✉ Chinese University, Sha Tin ☎ 2609 7416
🕐 Mon–Sat 10–4:30; Sun 12:30–4:30. Closed some holidays 🚇 University, then shuttle bus

KOWLOON PARK
For a short wander or a rest in between shopping trips, try this little oasis of peace and quiet. There's a statue collection, an aviary, a children's playground, some fountains, and plenty of people to watch.
✚ F6 ✉ Nathan Road, Tsim Sha Tsui 🚇 Tsim Sha Tsui

THE HONG KONG RACING MUSEUM
This museum at the Happy Valley racecourse charts Hong Kong's love of horse-racing since the track's foundation in 1884.
✚ G9 ✉ 2/F Happy Valley Stand Happy Valley Racecourse ☎ 2966 8065 🕐 Tue–Sat 10–6; Sun and public holidays 1–5. Race days 10–12:30. Closed Mon
🚋 Happy Valley tram from Central

POLICE MUSEUM
Exhibitions concerning the history of the Hong Kong police force, triads and narcotics.
✚ F9 ✉ 27 Coombe Road, Wan Chai Gap ☎ 2849 7019
🕐 Wed–Sun 9–5; Tue 2–5. Closed Mon 🚌 Bus 15 from Exchange Square

Just looking

There are plenty of places in Hong Kong where you can have some fun for free. It costs nothing to stand in one of the street markets and watch the strange mix of modern bustle and ancient tradition that goes on all around you. Several small museums, including the Railway Museum in Tai Po, Flagstaff House in Hong Kong Park, and the Sheung Yiu Folk Museum in Saiking, are free.

Kowloon Park

59

JOURNEYS

Stairway to heaven

Special to Hong Kong is the 15-minute trip up to the Mid Levels on escalators. The series of escalators begins in Central, on Des Voeux Road beside the Market, and carries on through the heart of the city and into suburbia. The covered escalators and walkways are on stilts above the streets, giving a fascinating insight into the life below.

> See Top 25 Sights for
> **PEAK TRAM ➤ 27**
> **STANLEY BY BUS NO. 6 OR 260 ➤ 48**
> **STAR FERRY ➤ 38**

FERRY TO CHEUNG CHAU

An air-conditioned first-class cabin with a bar and a sunny, open-air deck make this 40-minute ride past speeding catamarans, scruffy sampans, vast tankers and tiny golden islands a rare and relaxing treat.
➕ D7 ✉ Outlying Islands Ferry Pier, Central 🕐 Half-hourly 6:30AM–11:30PM 🚇 Central 💲 Moderate

HELICOPTER RIDES

Surely the ultimate in sightseeing, or at least it ought to be at these prices – HK\$7,470 for five passengers on a half-hour flight around Kowloon and the New Territories. Other rides can be negotiated.
➕ E8 ✉ Heliservices, 2 Ice House Street, Central ☎ 2802 0200 🕐 By arrangement 🚇 Central 💲 Expensive

Tram 8 to Kennedy Town

SHEK O BY BUS NO 9

The bus starts its journey at the end of the tram line in Shau Kei Wan, which was once a tiny fishing village but is now a suburb of the city. It gradually leaves civilisation behind as it heads out east along Shek O Road, past Tai Tam Bay with the South China Sea beyond and green hills inland.
➕ M8 ✉ Bus terminus, Nam On Street, Shau Kei Wan 🕐 Every 15–30 minutes 🚇 Shau Kei Wan 💲 Cheap

TRAM RIDE

This has to be one of the best value-for-money rides in the world. For HK\$1.60 you can travel the length of Hong Kong Island from Kennedy Town in the west to Shau Kei Wan in the east. The trams are double-decker, the top deck providing a bird's-eye view of the teeming life of Hong Kong Island.
➕ D7/M8 ✉ Central, Wan Chai ➕ Sheung Wan, Shau Kei Wan MTR 🕐 6AM–1AM 💲 Cheap

HONG KONG
where to...

CANTONESE FOOD

Prices

Approximate prices for a meal for two, excluding drinks

£££ over HK$600

££ HK$300 – HK$600

£ under HK$300

Dim sum

The most traditional of Cantonese meals, *dim sum* (literally 'small heart'), is served from early morning to late afternoon. The dishes – including steamed dumplings stuffed with a variety of meat and vegetable fillings – arrive in bamboo baskets piled high on a tray or trolley. As the servers circulate with the trolleys, just point at whatever takes your fancy. Popular dumplings include *har gau* (shrimps), *pai kwat* (spareribs) and *woo kok* (vegetarian), and you pay according to how many dishes you consume; the average price per dish is around HK$25.

BAMBOO VILLAGE FISHERMAN'S WHARF (££)

The decor evokes the traditional floating restaurants that were once common in the sheltered waters of the harbour. The speciality is seafood, but the menu is wide-ranging and includes dishes from other parts of Asia.

F8 ⊠ Shop 3–10, G/F, Tonnochy Towers, 250–274 Jaffe Road, Wan Chai ☎ 2827 1188 🕒 Mon–Sat 11AM–3PM, 11PM–5AM; Sun 10:30AM–5AM 🚇 Wan Chai

BROADWAY SEAFOOD RESTAURANT (£)

Specialities include scallops with black-bean sauce and crab fried with ginger, but there are also tasty chicken dishes. *Dim sum* served until 5PM.

F8 ⊠ Hay Wah Building, 73–85B Hennessy Road, Wan Chai ☎ 2529 9233 🕒 Daily 11AM–midnight 🚇 Wan Chai

DIAMOND RESTAURANT (£)

Affordable prices contribute to the popularity of this restaurant, while the noisy chatter at lunchtime is very characteristic of a *dim sum* restaurant. During the evening, the atmosphere is more sedate.

D8 ⊠ 267–75 Des Voeux Road, Central ☎ 2544 4708 🕒 Daily 6:30AM–11PM 🚇 Sheung Wan

JUMBO PALACE FLOATING RESTAURANT (£££)

The highly decorated boat – a tourist attraction in itself – adds to the spectacle of a night out that begins with a free ferry across the harbour in small sampan. *Dim sum* served from 7AM to 5PM.

Off map to south ⊠ Shun Wan, Wong Chuk Hang, Aberdeen ☎ 2554 0513 🕒 Daily 7AM–11PM 🚌 Bus 7 or 70 from Central Bus Terminal

LAI CHING HEEN (£££)

Cantonese cuisine at its very best (and at its priciest); novices cannot go wrong with the set dinner for two. The restaurant looks out across the harbour and the atmosphere – for a Chinese restaurant – is uncharacteristically subdued.

F7 ⊠ Regent Hotel, Salisbury Road, Tsim Sha Tsui ☎ 2721 1211 🕒 Daily noon–2:30, 6–11:30 🚇 Tsim Sha Tsui MTR

MAN WAH (£££)

Unlike most Chinese restaurants, the Man Wah is dimly lit, intimate and elegant, as you would expect in one of Hong Kong's best hotels. The food is excellent and worth the money.

E8 ⊠ Mandarin Oriental Hotel, 5 Connaught Road, Central ☎ 2522 0111 🕒 Daily noon–3, 6–11 🚇 Central

OTHER CHINESE REGIONAL FARE

AMERICAN RESTAURANT (£–££)
A colourful Beijing-style restaurant, with a variety of tasty dishes from the cold north of the People's Republic.
🕂 F8 ✉ 20 Lockhart Road, Wan Chai ☎ 2527 7277 🕓 Daily 11:30–11:30 🚇 Wan Chai

GREAT SHANGHAI RESTAURANT (£)
Shanghainese food, originating in the colder north, does not consist of lightly stir-fried Cantonese-like dishes. Cold smoked fish is a traditional starter, and fish dishes, especially eels, are a firm favourite for the main course. Reasonable prices, friendly service.
🕂 F6 ✉ 26 Prat Avenue, Tsim Sha Tsui ☎ 2366 8158 🕓 Daily 11–11 🚇 Tsim Sha Tsui

JUMBO FLOATING RESTAURANT (£)
This sister ship to the more expensive Jumbo Palace is good fun, especially at night, when the harbour sparkles from the restaurant's roof garden.
🕂 Off map to south ✉ Shum Wan, Wong Chuk Hang, Aberdeen ☎ 2553 9111 🕓 Daily 7:30AM–11:30PM 🚌 Bus 7 or 70 from Central Bus Terminal

NEW HOME HAKKA AND SEAFOOD RESTAURANT (£)
The nomadic Hakka came originally from the north of China; here you can dine on their dishes (such as beancurd and salt-baked chicken) rarely found outside China.
🕂 F6 ✉ 19–20 Hanoi Road, Tsim Sha Tsui ☎ 2366 5876 🕓 Daily 7AM–midnight 🚇 Tsim Sha Tsui

PRINCE COURT RESTAURANT (££)
The menu does not distinguish Cantonese from spicy Szechuan dishes, so ask for help when choosing. Favourite options include the seafood and beancurd soup, and the chilli prawns and noodles that carry a mouth-tingling bite.
🕂 F6 ✉ Shop 305, The Gateway, 25 Canton Road, Tsim Sha Tsui ☎ 2730 9131 🕓 Daily 11:30AM–midnight 🚇 Tsim Sha Tsui

SICHUAN GARDEN RESTAURANT (££)
The classic speciality of Szechuan food – a cuisine noted for its subtle use of spices – is smoked duck and it is available here.
🕂 D8 ✉ 3/F, Gloucester Tower, The Landmark, 11 Pedder Street, Central ☎ 2521 4433 🕓 Daily 11:30–3, 5:30–11:30 🚇 Central

SZE CHUEN LAU RESTAURANT (££)
This comfortable old-style Szechuan specialist offers smoked duck and other favourites.
🕂 G8 ✉ G/F 466 Lockhart Road, Causeway Bay ☎ 2891 9027 🕓 Daily noon–midnight 🚇 Causeway Bay

Handling chopsticks

- Hold one chopstick between thumb joint and tip of third finger
- Hold the other chopstick between tip of thumb and tips of first and second fingers
- Keep the first chopstick rigid while moving the second one up and down to pick up the food
- Put food from the serving dish on top of rice, hold the bowl close to your mouth and push the food in with the help of the chopsticks. Chinese etiquette does not demand precision and making a bit of a mess is quite acceptable.

PAN-ASIAN CUISINES

Drinks

Hotel restaurants and cafés are best for non-Chinese tea with fresh milk and sugar. For decent coffee look for the European- and American-style coffee booths in glitzy shopping centres. Foreign beers and spirits are readily available – try *Tsingrao*, a sharp-tasting Chinese beer inspired by a German recipe. If you are not used to the local beer, *San Miguel*, you may find it gives you a bad hangover. Western wine is available in most restaurants.

FELIX (££)

Excellent Californian/Pan-Asian cuisine in a modern restaurant designed by Philippe Starck. Check out the chairs and, for males, the toilets!

F8 ✉ Peninsula Hotel, Salisbury Road, Kowloon ☎ 2366 6251 🕐 Daily 11:30–3, 6:30–11 🚇 Tsim Shu Tsui MTR

INDOCHINE (££–£££)

The French influence on Vietnamese food is very apparent in the menu of this trendy restaurant that serves up its dishes in an airy laid-back setting.

D8 ✉ 2/F, California Tower, 30–32 D'Aguilar Street, Central ☎ 2869 7399 🕐 Daily noon–3, 7–midnight 🚇 Central

INTERNATIONAL CURRY HOUSE (£)

A wide range of curries from across South-East Asia and the Indian sub-continent. Suitable for meat-eaters and vegetarians.

F9 ✉ G/F, 26–28 Tai Wong Street East, Wan Chai ☎ 2529 0088 🕐 Daily noon–midnight 🚇 Wan Chai

JAVA RIJSTTAFEL RESTAURANT (£)

Indonesian favourites such as *gado gado* (mixed vegetables) and *satay* are the staple. The evening *rijsttafel* (rice table) buffet provides a good introduction to this popular cuisine with chilli-inspired thrills complemented by the soothing coconut taste.

F6 ✉ G/F, Han Hing Mansion, 38 Hankow Road, Tsim Sha Tsui ☎ 2367 1230 🕐 Daily noon–10:30 🚇 Tsim Sha Tsui

MABUHAY RESTAURANT (£)

A friendly little restaurant that serves authentic Filipino and Spanish dishes at reasonable prices.

F6 ✉ 11 Minden Avenue, Tsim Sha Tsui ☎ 2367 3762 🕐 Daily 8:30AM–11PM 🚇 Tsim Sha Tsui

STANLEY'S ORIENTAL RESTAURANT (££)

Cajun, Creole, Japanese, Thai and Indian. Beach-front location is perfect for a leisurely meal; the fan-cooled veranda offers the best views .

Off map to south-east ✉ 90B Stanley Main Street, Stanley ☎ 2813 9988 🕐 Daily 9AM–midnight 🚌 Bus 6 or 260 from Central Bus Terminal

SUPATRA'S THAI GOURMET (££)

Weekday lunch buffet. At night, choose a window table to watch trendy Lan Kwai Fong at play or go upstairs for a more formal meal.

D8 ✉ 50 D'Aguilar Street, Central ☎ 2522 5073 🕐 Sun–Thu noon–midnight; Fri–Sat noon–3AM 🚇 Central

VICEROY BAR AND RESTAURANT (££)

Indian, Thai and Indonesian, the Indian dishes are best. Ask for a table outside.

F8 ✉ 2/F, Sun Hung Kai Centre, 30 Harbour Road, Wan Chai ☎ 2827 7777 🕐 Daily noon–3, 6–11:30 🚇 Wan Chai

JAPANESE FOOD

AH-SO (£)
Authentic Japanese-style design with U-shaped *sushi* bar serving crispy *tempura* and fried prawns as well as a range of raw fish. Service is fast, and patrons are not expected to sit around for long after eating. Enjoyable.
➕ E6 ✉ 159 Craigie Court, World Finance Centre, Harbour City, Canton Road, Tsim Sha Tsui ☎ 2730 3392 🕐 Daily noon–3, 5–11 🚇 Tsim Sha Tsui

GANRUK (£)
Typically Japanese in that space is limited – but this is good-value Japanese food. Don't bother with reservations; just avoid weekends if you want elbow room.
➕ F6 ✉ 27a Chatham Road South, Tsim Sha Tsui ☎ 2369 9728 🕐 Daily 11–11 🚇 Tsim Sha Tsui

HANAGUSHI JAPANESE RESTAURANT (££)
Yakitori (grilled meat on skewers) is the speciality of this friendly little restaurant and is always in the set meals as well as on the menu.
➕ D8 ✉ 101–2 California Entertainment Building, 34–6 D'Aguilar Street, Central ☎ 2521 0868 🕐 Mon–Fri 10:30–3, 6–11:30; Sat 11–3, 6–11:30. Closed Sun 🚇 Central

MOMOYAMA JAPANESE RESTAURANT (£££)
Most customers are happy with the set meals offered at dinner and lunch. Quieter in the evening and more space at the *sushi* counter.
➕ E8 ✉ LG/F, Jardine House, 1 Connaught Place, Central ☎ 2845 8773 🕐 Daily 11–3, 5:30–10:30 🚇 Central

SAGANO RESTAURANT (£££)
Japanese chefs in a Japanese hotel with imported Japanese food; the speciality is *kansai* cuisine from the Kyoto area. The scene through the huge harbour-facing window competes with that of the *teppanyaki* counter where chefs juggle with their cooking tools.
➕ G6 ✉ Hotel Nikko, 72 Mody Road, Tsim Sha Tsui ☎ 2739 1111 🕐 Daily 7–9:30, noon–2:30, 6–10:30 🚇 Tsim Sha Tsui

UNKAI JAPANESE RESTAURANT (££)
One of the better-value hotel restaurants, where Japanese chefs produce authentic dishes and waitresses dress in traditional style. Set meals are the best value.
➕ F6 ✉ 3/F, Sheraton Hotel, 20 Nathan Road, Tsim Sha Tsui ☎ 2369 1111 ext 2 🕐 Daily noon–2:30, 6:30–10:30 🚇 Tsim Sha Tsui

YOROHACHI JAPANESE RESTAURANT (££)
A good place to enjoy traditional *tempura*, *teppanyaki* or *sushi*. The set meals are reasonably priced.
➕ D8 ✉ 5–6 Lan Kwai Fong, Central ☎ 2524 1251 🕐 Daily 11–3, 6–11 🚇 Central

Which dish?
If you are unfamiliar with Japanese food, start with one of the set meals. Raw fish comes either as *sushi* (wrapped in rice or seaweed) or *sashimi* (in slices with a horseradish sauce for dipping), or try *tempura* (deep-fried fish and vegetables) or *teppanyaki* (grilled meat and seafood). Many Japanese department stores have inexpensive cafés that serve most of the above.

INDIAN DINING

Vegetarian choice

Vegetarians tend to look to South Indian restaurants, which don't usually serve meat but, although meaty North Indian establishments are more common in Hong Kong, vegetarians are rarely disappointed. A couple of green vegetable dishes accompanied by *raita* (yoghurt) and *naan* (wholewheat puffed-up bread baked in an oven), not forgetting a lentil *dal*, and two people will have a small feast to savour.

THE ASHOKA RESTAURANT (£)

Delicious curries and tandoori dishes; some vegetarian, all tasty and spicy.

�� D8 ✉ G/F, 57 Wyndham Street, Central ☎ 2524 9623; ⏰ Daily noon–2:30, 6–10:30 🚇 Central
Also at
🔗 F8 ✉ Shop 1,G/F, Connaught Commercial Building, 185 Wan Chai Road, Wan Chai ☎ 2891 8981 ⏰ Daily noon–2:30, 6–10:30 🚇 Wan Chai

DELHI CLUB MESS (£)

Plush by Chungking Mansions standards (► 86, panel), frequented by regulars – two good reasons for an affordable feast here.

🔗 F6 ✉ Block C, Flat 3, 3/F, Chungking Mansions, 36–44 Nathan Road, Tsim Sha Tsui ☎ 2368 1682 ⏰ Daily noon–3:30, 6–11:30 🚇 Tsim Sha Tsui

GAYLORD INDIAN RESTAURANT (££)

Superb appetisers; the breads and kebabs come fresh out of the tandoori oven. Daily lunch buffets. Cosy and pubby.

🔗 F6 ✉ 1/F, Ashley Centre, 23–5 Ashley Road, Tsim Sha Tsui ☎ 2376 1001 ⏰ Daily 11:45–3, 6–11:30 🚇 Tsim Sha Tsui

JO JO MESS CLUB (£)

Probably the least expensive place for consistently good food in Wan Chai.

🔗 F9 ✉ 86 Johnston Road (entrance on Lee Tung Street), Wan Chai ☎ 2527 3776 ⏰ Daily 11–3, 6–11 🚇 Wan Chai

KOH-I-NOOR (£)

A good bet for those seeking affordable meals on Hong Kong Island. The cuisine is North Indian but the spiciness is moderated; vegetarian dishes are on the menu.

🔗 D8 ✉ 1/F, 103 California Entertainment Building, 34 D'Aguilar Street, Central ☎ 2877 9706 ⏰ Daily 11:30–3, 6–11 🚇 Central

NANAK MESS (£)

No-frills whatever – but peaceful. Inexpensive, reliable, authentic and consistently tasty food.

🔗 F6 ✉ Block A, Flat 4,11/F, Chungking Mansions, 36–44 Nathan Road, Tsim Sha Tsui ☎ 2368 8063 ⏰ Daily noon–3, 7–11 🚇 Tsim Sha Tsui

TANDOOR RESTAURANT (££–£££)

A classy restaurant with rosewood furniture. Wide-ranging menu, with betelnut-based desserts being one of the specialities. Lunch and dinner buffets.

🔗 D8 ✉ 19 Wyndham Street, Central ☎ 2845 2299 ⏰ Daily noon–2:30, 6–10:45 🚇 Central

WOODLANDS INTERNATIONAL RESTAURANT (£)

The city's only Indian vegetarian restaurant; the *dosa* (rice-flour pancakes) and *thali* set meals are excellent and good value. No alcohol. Canteen-style decor.

🔗 F6 ✉ G/F, Mirror Tower, 61 Mody Road, Tsim Sha Tsui ☎ 2369 3718 ⏰ Daily noon–3:30, 6:30–11 🚇 Tsim Sha Tsui

AMERICAN & MEXICAN FARE

AL'S DINER (££)
Sirloin from the US is minced for the fair-sized burgers. There's lots of neon and a juke box churns out period songs.
➕ D8 ✉ Room F, G/F, Winner Building, 27–37 D'Aguilar Street, Central ☎ 2869 1869 🕐 Mon–Thu 11AM–12:30AM; Fri–Sat 11AM–3AM; Sun 6PM–12:30AM 🚇 Central

THE BOSTONIAN (£££)
The best of the menu offers fresh fish (brought to your table for choosing), plus the imaginative preparations and colourful decor suggest California cuisine – never mind the restaurant's name. If you come for the lunch buffet, plan for a light dinner.
➕ F6 ✉ Renaissance Hotel, 8 Peking Road, Tsim Sha Tsui ☎ 2375 1133 🕐 Daily noon–2:30, 7–11 🚇 Tsim Sha Tsui

CASA MEXICANA (££)
Tacos, enchiladas and steaks. The real fun, though, comes from the live music – you can dance on your chairs until you're ready to drop.
➕ H7 ✉ G/F Victoria Centre, 15 Watson Road, North Point ☎ 2566 5560 🕐 Daily 11:30AM–midnight 🚇 Fortress Hill

DAN RYAN'S CHICAGO GRILL (££)
Traditional favourites on the menu include clam chowder, potato skins, salads and the supreme baby back ribs in barbecue sauce. Leave room for the brownies or carrot cake. Be sure to book – this place is understandably popular.
➕ F6 ✉ 200 Ocean Terminal, Harbour City, Tsim Sha Tsui ☎ 2735 6111 🕐 Mon–Fri 11AM–midnight; Sat–Sun 10AM–midnight. Closes 2AM Fri 🚇 Tsim Sha Tsui
Also at
➕ E8 ✉ 114 Pacific Place, 88 Queensway, Central ☎ 2845 4600 🕐 Mon–Fri 11AM–midnight; Sat–Sun 10AM–midnight. Closes 2AM Sat 🚇 Admiralty

RUBY TUESDAY AMERICAN GRILL (£)
Fajitas, potato skins, *nachos*, ribs, burgers – plus tempting and colourful desserts.
➕ D8 ✉ UG/F (Shop A) and 2/F, Century Square, 1–13 D'Aguilar Street, Central ☎ 2537 9999 🕐 Daily 11:30AM–1AM 🚇 Central

SAN FRANCISCO STEAK HOUSE (££)
Rely on this well established restaurant for its huge steaks (imported from the US), as well as burgers and salads. The setting is comfortably old-fashioned and dimly lit, evoking early 20th-century San Francisco.
➕ F6 ✉ Basement of Bank of Tokyo building, corner of Ashley Road and Peking Road, Tsim Sha Tsui ☎ 2735 7576 🕐 Daily noon–midnight 🚇 Tsim Sha Tsui

Afternoon tea
The red pillar boxes have all been repainted green, but the British ritual of afternoon tea is still going strong. For the full works – chinaware, chandeliers and string quartets – the Peninsula Hotel in Salisbury Road (► 84, panel) is hard to beat, but the Grand Hyatt in Wan Chai and the Mandarin Oriental (► 84) are worthy and equally expensive alternatives.

EUROPEAN FOOD

Europe in Asia

Virtually every European cuisine is represented in Hong Kong and the quality of the food in the restaurants on these pages loses nothing from being transplanted from the Occident to the Orient. Local Chinese and Asian visitors like the more expensive hotel restaurants, while younger Hong Kong couples prefer the more informal European-style places.

Hotel restaurants

These tend to be the most expensive dining options in Hong Kong but the standard of service, the quality of food and choice of wines are usually excellent. The styles – both culinary and interior design – range from the ultra modern, such as Felix (► 64) to the highly conventional, like Gaddi's (see right).

AMIGO RESTAURANT (£££)
Spanish setting, French dishes (*filet de sole Marquis, crevettes au gruyère*). The set meals at lunchtime are cheaper and less formal.
✚ G9 ✉ Amigo Mansion, 79A Wong Nei Chung Road, Happy Valley ☎ 2577 2202 ⏰ Daily noon–3, 6–midnight 🚃 Tram from Central

BEACHES (£)
Mediterranean-style bar and eatery with outdoor tables overlooking Stanley Bay and music videos in the background. Pizza and pasta mostly.
✚ Off map to south ✉ G/F 92B Stanley Street, Stanley ☎ 2813 0993 ⏰ Fri–Sat 11AM–2AM; Sun–Thu 11AM–1AM 🚌 Bus 6 or 260 from Central Bus Terminal

THE CHALET (£££)
Timber, brick, stone and fondue – elemental Swiss setting and cuisine. Widest range of Swiss wines outside Europe.
✚ F6 ✉ 9/F, Royal Pacific Hotel, China Hong Kong City, 33 Canton Road, Tsim Sha Tsui ☎ 2738 2388 ⏰ Daily noon–2:30, 7–11 🚇 Tsim Sha Tsui

GADDI'S (£££)
One of Hong Kong's best restaurants – a place to remember, especially at night when the chandeliers are sparkling and the band is playing. Popular with Asian tourists for both service and the French food. Booking is essential.
✚ F6 ✉ 1/F, Peninsula Hotel, Salisbury Road, Tsim Sha Tsui ☎ 2366 6251 ⏰ Daily noon–3, 6:30–11 🚇 Tsim Sha Tsui

HUGO'S (£££)
Busy but still intimate, Hugo's is famous for its free gifts of roses and cigars. The Sunday brunch is a feast (booking is essential). In the evening, candlelight and serenaders create a mood of romance.
✚ F6 ✉ Hyatt Regency Hotel, 67 Nathan Road, Tsim Sha Tsui ☎ 2311 1234 ⏰ Mon–Sat noon–3, 7–11; Sun 11:30–3, 7–11 🚇 Tsim Sha Tsui

JIMMY'S KITCHEN (££)
Its history stretches back to the 1920s, venerable for Hong Kong, and its menu can be relied on for its signature *goulash, borscht, stroganoff*. Comfortable, traditional setting; service as reliable as the food.
✚ D8 ✉ Basement, South China Building, 1 Wyndham Street, Central ☎ 2526 5293 ⏰ Daily noon–midnight 🚇 Central

LA TAVERNA RESTAURANT (££)
Chianti bottles and checked tablecloths set the tone; a wide-ranging menu with a good choice of pasta dishes provides the sustenance. On Kowloon and Hong Kong Island.
✚ D8 ✉ G/F, Astoria Building, 34–8 Ashley Road, Tsim Sha Tsui ☎ 2523 8624 ⏰ Mon–Sat noon–3, 6:30–midnight; Sun 6:30–midnight 🚇 Central
Also at

➕ F6 ✉ 1/F, Shun Ho Tower, 24–30 Ice House Street, Central ☎ 2376 1945 🕐 Mon–Sat noon–3, 6:30–midnight; Sun 6:30–midnight 🚇 Tsim Sha Tsui

THE MISTRAL (£££)
Come for a relaxed meal and forget the crowds of Tsim Sha Tsui. Excellent pasta, pizza and other Italian dishes. Rustic Mediterranean setting makes you forget you're in a hotel.
➕ G6 ✉ Basement, Grand Stanford, Harbour View, 70 Mody Road, Tsim Sha Tsui East ☎ 2721 5161 🕐 Daily noon–3, 7–11 🚇 Tsim Sha Tsui

PIERROT (£££)
A top French restaurant with fine harbour views. Stylish presentation, impeccable service, and a caviar menu.
➕ E8 ✉ Mandarin Oriental Hotel, 5 Connaught Road, Central ☎ 2522 0111 🕐 Mon–Fri noon–3, 7–11; Sat, Sun 7–11 🚇 Central

THE PIZZERIA (££)
North Italian pasta and dishes. Good selection of regional wines.
➕ F6 ✉ 2/F, Kowloon Hotel, 19–21 Nathan Road, Tsim Sha Tsui ☎ 2369 8698 ext 3322 🕐 Daily 11:45–3, 6–11 🚇 Tsim Sha Tsui

POMEROY'S WINE BAR (££)
In a prominent shopping centre. When offices close around 5PM, *gweilos* line up at the bar. Fish and chips, pasta, burgers, salad – and quick service.
➕ E8 ✉ Shop 349, Level 3, The Mall, Pacific Place Two, 88 Queensway, Central ☎ 2523 4772 🕐 Daily 11AM–midnight 🚇 Admiralty

THE PORTO (££)
The best Portuguese cuisine in Hong Kong, as good as any in Macau. Delicacies like *pasteis de bacalhau* and standards like *chourico* sausage and African chicken.
➕ F4 ✉ 1/F, Metropole Hotel, 75 Waterloo Road, Mong Kok ☎ 2761 1711 🕐 Daily noon–3, 6:30–11:30 🚇 Mong Kok

LA RONDA (££)
The better of the city's two revolving restaurants; on the 30th floor. A huge international buffet mixes oriental with occidental fare. Booking essential.
➕ E8 ✉ 30/F, Hotel Furama Kempinksi, Connaught Road, Central ☎ 2525 5111 🕐 Daily noon–3PM, 6–11PM 🚇 Central MTR

SAMMY'S KITCHEN (£)
Named after the Chinese chef famous for his snails, flambées and other European dishes.
➕ C7 ✉ G/F, 204–6 Queen's Road West, Sheung Wan ☎ 2548 8400 🕐 Daily 11:30–11:30 🚇 Sheung Wan

STANLEY'S FRENCH RESTAURANT (££)
A modern European menu specialising in seafood. The veal is also delicious. Book for terrace and roof tables.
➕ Off map to south ✉ 86 Stanley Main Street, Stanley ☎ 2813 8873 🕐 Daily 9–9 🚌 Bus 6 or 260 from Central Bus Terminal

Rooms with a view
The best two rooms with a view are Parc 27 (✉ Park Lane Hotel, 310 Gloucester Road, Causeway Bay ☎ 2890 3350) and La Ronda (✉ Hotel Furama Kempinski, 1 Connaught Road, Central ☎ 2525 5111).

ARTS & CRAFTS

The HKTA

Look out for the HKTA logo in shop windows. It means that the shop is registered with the Hong Kong Tourist Association and is committed to certain standards – that is, it will promptly rectify complaints and give you adequate value for money. More importantly, at these shops the HKTA will investigate and help you get redress if you choose to bring a complaint (although it does not accept liability for the behaviour of its registered members).

CHINA PRODUCTS

Similar to the other China Products stores, but offers a 15 per cent discount to foreigners.
🔶 G8 ✉ 488–500 Hennessy Road, Causeway Bay ☎ 2577 0222 🕐 Daily 10–8
🚇 Causeway Bay

CHINESE ARTS AND CRAFTS (HK) LTD

Beautiful things, ranging from pottery to silks, embroideries, carved gemstones, clothes, furniture, carpets, tea, jewellery, statues and novelties.
🔶 F6 ✉ Star House, 3 Salisbury Road, Tsim Sha Tsui
☎ 2375 4061 🕐 Daily 10–8. Closed Chinese New Year
🚇 Tsim Sha Tsui

CHINESE ARTS AND CRAFTS (HK) LTD

Compared to the other Chinese emporia, more designer rosewood and lacquer furniture, lamps and carpets.
🔶 F8 ✉ Lower Block, China Resources Building, 26 Harbour Road, Wan Chai ☎ 2827 6667
🕐 Daily 10–8 🚇 Wan Chai

LUK'S FURNITURE

Three floors of rosewood furniture, chests from Korea and lacquerware. Some items are small enough to put in a suitcase, or the shop will pack and post larger purchases for you. Worth the trip out to Aberdeen.
✉ GF–3F Aberdeen Harbour Mansion, 52–64 Aberdeen Main Road, Aberdeen ☎ 2553 4125
🕐 Mon–Sat 9:30–6, Sun 11–5
🚌 Bus 7 or 70 from Central Bus Terminal

MOUNTAIN FOLKCRAFT

Handmade craftwork such as paintings, carvings and batik from countries around South-East Asia.
🔶 D8 ✉ 12 Wo On Lane, Central ☎ 2525 3199
🕐 Mon–Sat 9:30–6:30
🚇 Central

STANLEY CHINESE PRODUCTS CO LTD

This is one of several good stalls and shops around Stanley Market, all offering embroideries, gift items, clothes and silks at competitive prices. Bargaining might not go amiss here.
🔶 Off map to south ✉ 22–26 Stanley Main Street, Stanley
☎ 2813 0649 🕐 Daily 10–6:30 🚌 Bus 6 from Central Bus Terminal

YUE HWA CHINESE PRODUCTS EMPORIUM

A much more basic and everyday kind of shop than the more centrally located Chinese emporia. Beautiful yet inexpensive dinner services, embroideries, expensive and inexpensive jewellery, workaday silk items and Chinese herbal medicines.
🔶 F5 ✉ 301 Nathan Road, Kowloon ☎ 2384 0084
🕐 Daily 10–10 🚇 Jordan

ANTIQUES

AMAZING GRACE ELEPHANT CO

Antiques, curios and gift items from around Asia. Branches in Excelsior Hotel shopping centre, Causeway Bay, and City Plaza, Tai Koo Shing.

🗺 F6 ✉ 348–9 Ocean Centre, Harbour City, Tsim Sha Tsui ☎ 2730 5455 🕓 Daily 9:30–7:30 🚇 Tsim Sha Tsui

THE BANYAN TREE LTD

Antiques, arts and crafts. Furniture from India, the Philippines, Indonesia and South America. Another branch in the shopping arcade in Repulse Bay.

🗺 F6 ✉ Room 257, Ocean Terminal, Canton Road, Tsim Sha Tsui ☎ 2730 6631 🕓 Mon–Sat 10:30–7, Sun 12:30–7 🚇 Tsim Sha Tsui

CAT STREET GALLERIES

A whole shopping centre full of antiques dealers and curio shops, close to the Hollywood Road antiques area.

🗺 D8 ✉ 38 Lok Ku Road, Sheung Wan ☎ 2541 8908 🕓 Daily 10–6 🚇 Sheung Wan

CHARLOTTE HORSTMAN AND GERALD GODFREY

Antiques from Asia – furniture and giftware. The fine mix includes modern craft items, but the specialty is bronze-ware, woodcarvings and furniture. Shipping can be arranged.

🗺 F6 ✉ Deck 1, Ocean Terminal, Tsim Sha Tsui ☎ 2735 7167 🕓 Daily 10–8 🚇 Tsim Sha Tsui

HONEYCHURCH ANTIQUES

Antique silver, utensils, jewellery and ornaments from around the world, including the UK and Asia.

🗺 D8 ✉ 29 Hollywood Road, Central ☎ 2543 2433 🕓 Mon–Sat 10–6 🚇 Central

REGALIA ART TREASURES

Some very pretty pieces of modern and antique wooden furniture, especially Korean chests, lacquered furniture and boxes.

🗺 F7 ✉ B1–36 New World Shopping Centre, 18–24 Salisbury Road, Tsim Sha Tsui ☎ 2369 6978 🕓 Daily 10:30–7:30 🚇 Tsim Sha Tsui

WAH TUNG CHINA CO

Several storeys of wonderful pots, old and new – both individual pieces and whole, Western- or Chinese-style dinner services Smaller branch in Hollywood Road.

🗺 Off map to south ✉ 14–17/F, Grand Marine Industrial Building, 3 Yue Fung Street, off Shek Pai Wan Road, Tin Wan, Aberdeen ☎ 2873 2272 🕓 Mon–Sat 9:30–6; Sun 11–5 🚌 Bus 7 or 70 from Central

YUE PO CHAI ANTIQUES

This long-established shop is worth a browse for its enormous range of antiques and curios.

🗺 D8 ✉ G/F, 132–6 Hollywood Road, Central ☎ 2540 4374 🕓 Daily 9–6 🚇 Central

Hollywood Road

If you are a serious antique collector or just like browsing among junk and curios, a major destination on your itinerary has to be Hollywood Road. The antiques shops start at the beginning of the road and continue for about a mile, incorporating Upper Lascar Row, which is a real flea market. Antiques that are more than 100 years old must have a certificate of authenticity. If you plan to spend a lot you might want to check with your consulate first to find out if there will be duty charges.

JEWELLERY & WATCHES

A gem of a place

There are more jewellery shops per head of the population in Hong Kong than in any other country. In additioin to jade and pearls, there are many semi-precious stones available and lots of silver jewellery from around Asia. Diamonds here should cost about 10 per cent less than elsewhere – Hong Kong is one of the world's biggest diamond markets. The market at Stanley is a good place to shop for silver and beads, while any shop displaying the Hong Kong Tourist Association (HKTA) sign (► 70, panel) is a relatively safe bet for more expensive items.

CARTIER'S

Just one of the many classy designer jewellery shops in Hong Kong. Prices are lower than in other parts of the world.
✚ F6 ⊠ Peninsula Hotel, Salisbury Road, Tsim Sha Tsui ☎ 2368 8036 ⊙ Daily 10–7 ⊡ Tsim Sha Tsui

CHINESE ARTS AND CRAFTS SHOPS

These shops have extensive jewellery departments selling watches and jewellery, particularly jade and gold items.
► 70 for details

CHOW TAI FOOK

This is just one branch of a good local jewellery chain that has branches in Causeway Bay, Central and around Mong Kok. It is a good place to shop for jade and to watch local people going about the serious business of buying.
✚ D8 ⊠ G2 China Building, Queen's Road, Central ☎ 2523 7128 ⊙ Daily 10–7:30 ⊡ Central

INTERNATIONAL PEARL CENTRE

As you would expect, you'll find pearls here, and there are also diamonds.
✚ F6 ⊠ G/F, Hankow Centre, 49 Peking Road, Tsim Sha Tsui ☎ 2366 4660 ⊙ Tue–Sun 10–7:30, Mon 10–5:30 ⊡ Tsim Sha Tsui

KAI YIN LO LTD

Original Hong Kong jewellery designs with an oriental flavour. There is a branch in the Mandarin Oriental Shopping Arcade, Central.
✚ E8 ⊠ Shop 373, The Mall, Pacific Place, 88 Queensway, Central ☎ 2840 0066 ⊙ Mon–Sat 9:30–6:30, Sun 1–6 ⊡ Admiralty

KS SZE & SONS LTD

A good excuse to see inside the Mandarin Oriental Hotel. This shop sells jewellery with an emphasis on pearls and a commitment to fair prices.
✚ E8 ⊠ Shop M11, Mandarin Oriental Hotel, 5 Connaught Road, Central ☎ 2524 2803 ⊙ Mon–Sat 9:30–6. Closed Sun ⊡ Central

LARRY JEWELLERY

One of several branches of the internationally famous jeweller.
✚ E8 ⊠ Shop 232, Level 2, The Mall, Pacific Place Two, 88 Queensway, Central ☎ 2868 3993 ⊙ Daily 10–7 ⊡ Admiralty

OPAL MINE

This is both a shop and an exhibition about opal mining and processing. Prices are low because precious stones are not taxed when they are imported into Hong Kong.
✚ F6 ⊠ G/F, Burlington House, 92 Nathan Road, Tsim Sha Tsui ☎ 2721 9933 ⊙ Daily 9:30–6:30 ⊡ Tsim Sha Tsui

COMPUTERS

COMPUTER MALL

A collection of specialist computer shops retailing hardware and software. More glitzy, comfortable and sophisticated looking than the shops in Sham Shui Po, but basically the products for sale are the same. Not all staff are equally knowledgeable so make sure you know your requirements.

🔲 G8 ✉ 11–12/F, The In Square, Windsor House, 311 Gloucester Road, Causeway Bay ⏰ Daily 10–8 🚇 Causeway Bay

GOLDEN SHOPPING CENTRE

A few shops sell computer books in English. At the MTR station follow the exit for the Golden Shopping Centre; it is the shabby-looking building directly across the road. Once Hong Kong residents' favourite source of pirated software, the basement of this centre still has the occasional fly-by-night shop.

🔲 E2 ✉ Golden Shopping Centre, 146–52 Fuk Wa Street, Sham Shui Po ⏰ Daily 11–8 🚇 Sham Shui Po

MONG KOK COMPUTER CENTRE

This small shopping block is crammed with tiny shops that spill out into the teeming corridors. The vendors are knowledgeable and catalogues of prices are on display. It specialises in Asian-made hardware: computers,
monitors, printers and add-on boards. Warranties are usually only for the Asian region but prices are very competitive.

🔲 F4 ✉ Mong Kok Computer Centre, 8–8a Nelson Street, Mong Kok ☎ 2740 9919 ⏰ Daily 11–8 🚇 Mong Kok

NEW CAPITAL COMPUTER PLAZA

The concentration of computer shops here is far less dense than at the nearby Golden Shopping Centre. Discounts of 10–20 per cent on software can often be negotiated.

🔲 E2 ✉ 100–2 Yen Chow Street, Sham Shui Po ⏰ Daily 11–8 🚇 Sham Shui Po

THE NOTEBOOK SHOP

The entire second floor of Star House, known as Star Computer City, is devoted to computers and peripherals. This particular shop stocks only laptop computers, including quality names such as Toshiba and IBM. Special offers are usually available.

🔲 F6/F7 ✉ Unit A6–7, 2/F, Star House, 3 Salisbury Road, Tsim Sha Tsui ☎ 2736 7260 ⏰ Mon–Fri 9:30–6:30; Sat 9:30–5:30. Closed Sun. 🚇 Tsim Sha Tsui

Shopping tips

Before parting with any money check whether the warranty is an international one or just for Asia. If the latter, the price should be lower. Always check a quote with other retailers before making a substantial purchase. When buying software, ensure that your hardware meets the minimum memory and speed requirements. Prices in Hong Kong are comparable to those in the US; Europeans will find some good bargains.

73

CAMERAS & ELECTRONICS

Shopping tips

Prices in Hong Kong for cameras and electronics are pretty much equivalent to those in Europe and possibly higher than in the US. Before you leave home check prices on the kinds of items you may be tempted to buy. Second, shop only at stores that display the Hong Kong Tourist Association (HKTA) sign (see ➤ 70, panel) and avoid shops in Tsim Sha Tsui that do not display prices. Third, get prices from various dealers and try haggling a little. Finally, if you do make a purchase, use a credit card, and watch carefully as your acquisition is put back into its box and then into a bag — many dealers won't take stuff back after you've left the store.

BROADWAY PHOTO SUPPLY

This is the biggest branch of a Hong Kong-wide electronics and electrical chain which sells everything from washing machines to electric razors. Most major brands are available at marked down prices, which are more or less fixed, although you might get a free gift thrown in. You can get a good idea here of a sensible local price, and then move on to serious haggling in some smaller, pushier place if you really want to.

➕ F4 ✉ G/F and 1/F, 731 Nathan Road, Mong Kok ☎ 2394 3827 ⏰ Mon–Sat 10:30–9:30; Sun 11:30–9:30 Ⓜ Mong Kok

FORTRESS

A major rival of Broadway offering a similar range of cameras, sound equipment, camcorders, electronics, electronic games and so on, all at fixed prices. There is a branch in Mong Kok, which is probably a bit bigger and has more on display, but this one is good for reconnaissance before setting off on a major haggling trip. Buy here and enjoy a hassle-free holiday, but if you like the cut and thrust of bargaining then this should at least be your first stop.

➕ F6 ✉ Shop 281, Ocean Terminal, Canton Road, Tsim Sha Tsui ☎ 2735 8628 ⏰ Mon–Fri 10:30–7:30, Sat, Sun and holidays 10–8 Ⓜ Tsim Sha Tsui

PHOTO SCIENTIFIC

Has a great reputation for good if not cheap prices for camera equipment and is especially liked by professional users. No bargaining here, just pay up. This street has several other camera equipment shops, so if you want to shop around you don't have far to go.

➕ D8 ✉ G/F, 6 Stanley Street, Central ☎ 2522 1903 ⏰ Mon–Sat 9–7. Closed Sun Ⓜ Central

WILLIAM'S PHOTO SUPPLY

A major competitor of Photo Scientific, this shop also deals with the cognoscenti of taking pictures. Again, no great bargains, but if you are searching for that special something it might just be here. Besides cameras there is the usual range of binoculars and the like.

➕ D8 ✉ 138B Prince's Building, 10 Chater Road, Central ☎ 2522 8437 ⏰ Mon–Sat 10–6:30. Closed Sun Ⓜ Central

SHA TIN

An area out towards the racecourse, full of small electronics shops, as well as branches of the major electrical outlets. Prices are more likely to be marked and fixed. You might also try the two department stores, Seiyu and Yaohan. Don't go on a Sunday or you will find yourself among what seems like the entire population of the New Territories.

➕ Off map to north Ⓜ Sha Tin

MEN'S CLOTHES

ASCOT CHANG

A Hong Kong institution, specialising in shirt-making.

✚ F6 ✉ Peninsula Hotel, Tsim Sha Tsui ☎ 2367 8319 🕐 Mon–Sat 9–7; Sun 9–5 🚇 Tsim Sha Tsui

CAUSEWAY BAY

This is a major shopping area, less touristy than Central or Tsim Sha Tsui. Here are four Japanese department stores – Matsuzakaya, Mitsukoshi, Daimaru, and Sogo – all with several designer outlets, and the enormous Times Square (➤ 57). Marks & Spencer is here, as are all the local chain stores and Lane Crawford (a South-East Asian upmarket department store).

✚ G8 🚇 Causeway Bay

THE LANDMARK

Men's shops in this plaza include Gentlemen Givenchy, Hugo, Ballantyne Boutique, Basile, Etienne Aigner, Jaeger, Benetton, Lanvin, Missoni and the Swank Shop. Prices are lower than for the same names in Europe. However, in the nearby Pedder Building there are lots of factory outlets selling the same labels at even lower prices (➤ 77).
➤ 56 for details

OCEAN CENTRE

This and the connecting malls have branches of Carpe Diem, Ermenegildo Zegna, Francescati, Gentlemen Givenchy, Hugo, Swank Shop, as well as the local chain stores, such as Giordano, G2000 and U2, and an excellent branch of Marks & Spencer.

✚ F6 ✉ Harbour City, 5 Canton Road, Tsim Sha Tsui 🕐 Daily 10–8 🚇 Tsim Sha Tsui

PACIFIC PLACE

A collection of designer outlets and local chain stores. This mall has an Alfred Dunhill, Ermenegildo Zegna, Hugo, Swank Shop, plus a Marks & Spencer, Lane Crawford and several local retailers selling casual separates at basic prices.
➤ 56 for details.

SAM'S

Another Hong Kong institution, numbering the Duke of Kent among its clientele.

✚ F6 ✉ Burlington Arcade K, 92–4 Nathan Road, Tsim Sha Tsui ☎ 2367 9423 🕐 Mon–Sat 10:30–7:30, Sun 10–12 🚇 Tsim Sha Tsui

W W CHAN & SONS

Suits made by this very classy tailor (with prices to match) have a lifespan of about 20 years and will be altered free of charge during that time. Once they have your measurements, you can order another suit from home.

✚ F6 ✉ A2, 2/F, Burlington House, 94 Nathan Road, Tsim Sha Tsui ☎ 2366 9738 🕐 Mon–Sat 9–6. Closed Sun 🚇 Tsim Sha Tsui

Made to measure

Perhaps the most distinctive aspect of men's clothes in Hong Kong is the number and quality of tailors and the excellent prices of their products compared to almost anywhere else. If you intend to have a suit made while you are in Hong Kong you should make finding a tailor that you like a priority since the more time and fittings he can have, the better the suit will be. A good tailor can make a suit in as little as 24 hours, but a few days will yield a better, cheaper suit. Some tailors offer a mail order service. See Ascot Chang and WW Chan, left, and Irene Fashions ➤ 76.

WOMEN'S CLOTHES

Shop 'til you drop

The really swanky place to go for women's clothes is The Landmark, where every big European name is represented, including Versace, Issey Miyake, Armani, Hermes, Loewe and Nina Ricci. The other shopping centres (► 56–57) all have an interesting range of clothes and labels. Note that shops aimed more at the local market tend to stock smaller sizes and frillier styles. A similar problem arises with shoes, which stop at around UK size 5 (European 38).

CHINESE ARTS AND CRAFTS (HK) LTD, TSIM SHA TSUI

This shop sells the most glorious silk underwear, embroidered *cheong sams* and jackets, crocheted silk sweaters, shawls and kimonos. The quality cannot always be relied upon.
► 70 for details

IRENE FASHIONS

This well-respected ladies' tailor takes several days and at least two fittings to make a suit. Take along something you like and have it copied, or choose the material and pattern at the shop.
🚇 D8 ✉ Room 1102–3, 11/F Tung Chai Building, 86–90 Wellington Street, Central ☎ 2850 5635 🕐 Mon–Sat 9–6. Closed Sun 🚇 Central

PACIFIC PLACE

Very expensive designer wear in Lane Crawford and Seibu department stores, T-shirts in local chain stores such as U2 or Giordano. Cotton Collection sells attractive cotton dresses, and Jessica has some elegant but inexpensive outfits.
► 56 for details

STANLEY MARKET

This market is full of interesting stalls selling all sorts of things, including discounted Monsoon clothes, sportswear, Indian prints, silk garments, funny T-shirts and designer jeans.
🚇 Off map to south ✉ Stanley 🚌 Bus 6

or 260 from Central Bus Terminal

TIMES SQUARE

When you have finished in this shopping mall there is more shopping near by – in the streets around Causeway Bay, the three department stores and the Excelsior Hotel shopping arcade.
► 57 for details

TOKYU

This reasonably priced department store has a whole arcade of local designer boutiques as well as all the big names. Clothes range from inexpensive young-style casuals to classy, costly evening gowns, and there is also some good-quality sportswear.
🚇 F7 ✉ New World Shopping Centre, Salisbury Road, Tsim Sha Tsui ☎ 2722 0102 🕐 Daily 10–9 🚇 Tsim Sha Tsui

VINCENT SUM DESIGNS

A handicraft shop that stocks lots of interesting and pretty batik cloth as well as clothes made from ethnic prints.
🚇 D8 ✉ 15 Lyndhurst Terrace, Central ☎ 2542 2610 🕐 Daily 10–6 🚇 Central

VOGUE ALLEY

A whole shopping centre dedicated to local-designer boutiques. Predominantly young clothes.
🚇 G8 ✉ Paterson and Kingston Streets, Causeway Bay 🚇 Causeway Bay

FACTORY OUTLETS

AH CHOW FACTORY

Chinese pottery and tableware, often very good quality or seconds. Also in this area are clothing factory outlets such as Mia Fashions at 680 Castle Peak Road, well worth a look.

✚ C1 ✉ Block B, 7F, 1 and 2 Hong Kong Industrial Centre, Castle Peak Road, Lai Chi Kok ☎ 2745 1511 ⏰ Daily 10–6 Phone for appointment 🚇 Lai Chi Kok

DIANE FREIS FACTORY OUTLET

Well-known local designer's factory with dresses and evening gowns with genuine reductions of about 30 per cent.

✚ H5 ✉ 41 Man Yue Street, Hung Hom ☎ 2362 1760 ⏰ Mon–Sat 9:30–6:30. Closed Sun 🚇 Tsim Sha Tsui then taxi

FA YUEN STREET

Better known for its street market (▶ 55), this is also home to a series of factory outlet shops. Labels are usually cut out, but you can find Marks & Spencer, Laura Ashley, Gore-tex, Next, Saks, Victoria's Secret and many other European and US chain store clothes at at least 50 per cent reductions.

✚ F3 ✉ Fa Yuen Street, Mong Kok ⏰ Daily 10–6 🚇 Prince Edward

HUNG HOM

The Kaiser estates are two blocks of mainly clothing factories, many of which have shops inside. The factories make clothes for department stores all over the world and their shops sell seconds or overruns with the labels cut out. There are also jewellery outlets here. A Hong Kong Tourist Association (HKTA) leaflet lists the major factories and there are regular advertisements in the newspapers; look in the *South China Morning Post*.

✚ G5–H5 🚇 Tsim Sha Tsui then taxi

LAN KWAI FONG

Several boutiques and shops sell clothes at reduced prices in this area, notably CCC, Gat and Whispers; all stock some well-known names at good prices.

✚ D8 ✉ Central 🚇 Central

PEDDER BUILDING

This shopping centre has five floors of tiny shops, all with something worth poking around for. Not all are factory outlets, and some sell both regular designer stuff and discounted items, so browse carefully.

✚ D8 ✉ 12 Pedder Street, Central 🚇 Central

TIMOTHY FASHION

Both men's and women's clothes. Good buys depend on the season – woollen sweaters in autumn, silk shirts and dresses in summer.

✚ H5 ✉ Kaiser Estate, Phase 1, 41 Man Yue Street, Hung Hom ☎ 2362 2389 ⏰ Mon–Sat 9:30–6:30. Closed Sun 🚇 Tsim Sha Tsui then taxi

Bargain bazaars

There are two major areas to look for bargains – in the Pedder Building on Hong Kong Island for the really big names, and around the factories themselves in Hung Hom in Kowloon. Granville Road in Tsim Sha Tsui is another place full of small shops selling anything from rubbish to amazing bargains, but you have to be dedicated to find the really good things. What you are likely to find is samples, seconds and overruns, often with the labels cut out. Women's clothes come mainly in small sizes but larger bodies are sometimes catered for.

THEATRES

Bookings

By quoting your passport number, tickets for most venues can be reserved (or paid for by credit card) by telephone through computerised central offices called URBTIX (☎ 2743 9009) between 10AM and 8PM, and then collected at the theatre within a set period of time. Check the tourist literature (► 92) to see what is on. Ticket prices are usually very good value, varying from about HK$400 for a good seat at a top event to HK$60 for a lesser event. City Hall and the Arts Centre (both URBTIX centres) are good places to peruse the promotional posters.

FRINGE CLUB

The main venue for non-mainstream performance art as well as some interesting drama workshops. During the main Arts Festival (► 79) alternative offerings are usually hosted here.
➕ D8 ✉ 2 Lower Albert Road, Central ☎ 2521 7251
🚇 Central

GOETHE INSTITUTE

The German Cultural Institute organises regular films, exhibitions and events to do with German culture and language in the Hong Kong Arts Centre.
➕ F8 ✉ 14/F, Hong Kong Arts Centre, 2 Harbour Road, Wan Chai ☎ 2802 0088 🚇 Wan Chai

HONG KONG ACADEMY FOR PERFORMING ARTS

There are different-sized theatres plus an outdoor venue in this arts school located next to the Arts Centre. The Academy concentrates on classical dance, drama and music.
➕ F8 ✉ 1 Gloucester Road, Wan Chai ☎ 2824 2651
🚇 Wan Chai

HONG KONG ARTS CENTRE

Theatre and music of diverse kinds take place here and it is always worth checking to see what is on. Ticket prices tend to be lower than at the Cultural Centre or City Hall.
➕ F8 ✉ 2 Harbour Road, Wan Chai ☎ 2582 0200
🚇 Wan Chai

HONG KONG CITY HALL

There's a theatre, auditorium and recital hall hosting a wide variety of local and visiting artists within the City Hall.
➕ E8 ✉ Edinburgh Place, Central ☎ 2840 2921
🚇 Central

HONG KONG COLISEUM

This is the largest venue in Hong Kong for rock concerts and sporting events, with some 12,000 seats.
➕ G6 ✉ 9 Cheong Wan Road, Hung Hom, Kowloon ☎ 2765 9233 🚇 Tsim Sha Tsui then taxi

HONG KONG CULTURAL CENTRE

The premier location for orchestral music, ballet and theatre. There is usually an international event of one genre or another on the schedule.
➕ F7 ✉ Salisbury Road, Tsim Sha Tsui ☎ 2734 2009
🚇 Tsim Sha Tsui

SHA TIN TOWN HALL

The large grey Town Hall at this town in the New Territories has good acoustics, and frequently hosts international artists, especially orchestras. To get there, walk straight through the huge shopping centre and out the other side; the Town Hall is next to the library.
✉ New Town Plaza, Sha Tin ☎ 2694 2536 🚇 Sha Tin

CONCERTS & SHOWS

ARTS FESTIVAL
This highly recommended event lasts three weeks and features international orchestras, dance and theatre, from opera and classical music to jazz, and from folk dance to ballet. Successful theatre productions from Europe, Asia and the US also visit. Tickets are often available right up to the last day.
🕐 Mid-Jan–mid-Mar

CHINESE CULTURAL SHOWS
The best way to catch a performance of a traditional dance or one of the other classical Chinese art forms is to check with HKTA (the Hong Kong Tourist Association) (▶ 88–9). Performances range from acrobatics, puppetry and magic shows to martial arts and folk dancing. Venues all over the territory.

CHINESE OPERA AT TEMPLE STREET NIGHT MARKET
The largely amateur performances take place irregularly, most likely around Chinese festivals, but they are enthusiastic and lively. Songs are in Cantonese. Details from HKTA (▶ 88–9).
🚇 F5–6 ✉ Temple Street, Mong Kok 🚇 Mong Kok

FESTIVAL OF ASIAN ARTS
This biennial event (held in even-numbered years) provides an opportunity to see music, dance and theatre from Asia. Visitors should seize the chance to see performances that are rarely put on elsewhere.
🕐 Oct–Nov

HONG KONG CHINESE ORCHESTRA
Chinese orchestral music is tonally different to Western music and a performance that uses the full range of traditional Chinese instruments is well worth finding. Contact the HKTA (▶ 88–9) for schedules.

HONG KONG DANCE COMPANY
The cmpany has been choreographing traditional and new Chinese dances for over 25 years; a fascinating spectacle. Details from HKTA (▶ 88–9).

HONG KONG PHILHARMONIC ORCHESTRA
A large, well-established orchestra with members drawn from Hong Kong, Europe and North America. Regular performances, often at weekends, take place in the Cultural Centre and City Hall. Ticket prices increase when a prestigious conductor arrives from overseas.

INTERNATIONAL FILM FESTIVAL
New films from around the world. Evening tickets sell quickly but other screenings usually have seats available at short notice.
🕐 Late Mar–early Apr

Chinese opera
Dating back to the 12th century, this is a highly stylised but very energetic art form. The basic story lines follow the Chinese myths. Characters wear startling make-up and gorgeous clothes. Though the Cantonese songs and accompaniment are loud and discordant to Western ears, the acrobatics and swordfights can be stunning. If you find an opera to watch, you will know it is a genuine cultural experience, not geared to tourists. Watch it as a spectacle rather than a story. The audience chats, wanders about, and sometimes joins in.

SPORTS

Away from it all

If you stay in Hong Kong long enough — and this may be just days, or even hours — the need to escape the crowds and enjoy some recreation becomes irresistible. Take a jog along Bowen Road (► 16) at any time of the day, an early morning or late evening jog along the Waterfront Promenade in Tsim Sha Tsui (► 18), or a more strenuous run up Victoria Peak (► 27). The Hash House Harriers (☎ 2376 229) organise regular runs.

SWIMMING

There are sandy beaches with safe swimming, but they are over-crowded at weekends and pollution periodically closes some. The following have lifeguards between April and September; if no red flag is hoisted, take a plunge. Shark attack warnings are occasionally posted on the beaches.

CHEUNG SHA
✉ Lantau Island ➧ Outlying Islands Pier, Central, then bus from Silvermine Bay

DEEP WATER BAY
✉ South side of Hong Kong Island 🚌 Bus 7 from Central Bus Terminal to Aberdeen, then bus 73

LO SO SHING
✉ Lamma Island ➧ Outlying Islands Pier, Central

REPULSE BAY
✉ South side of Hong Kong Island 🚌 Bus 6 or 61 from Central

SHEK O
✉ Southeast side of Hong Kong Island 🚌 Bus 9 from Shau Kei Wan

SILVERSTRAND
✉ Sai Kung Peninsula, New Territories 🚇 Choi Hung then Bus 92 or taxi

STANLEY BEACH
✉ South side of Hong Kong Island 🚌 Bus 6 or 260 from Central Bus Terminal

SPORTS AND RECREATION TOUR
This tour visits the Clearwater Bay Golf and Country Club (see below) for golf, tennis, badminton, squash and swimming. Equipment hire and lunch included in the HK$330 charge.
✉ Hong Kong Tourist Association offices (► 88) ☎ 2801 7177 🕐 Tue and Fri

GOLF

CLEARWATER BAY GOLF AND COUNTRY CLUB
Featured in the HKTA *Sports and Recreation Tour* (see above), this is a par-70, 18-hole, pro championship course.
✉ Lot #227 in DD 241, Po Toi O, Sai Kung, New Territories ☎ 2719 5936 🕐 Mon–Fri 7:30–6 🚇 Choi Hung MTR, then bus 92 ⛳ Green fees HK$1,400

DISCOVERY BAY GOLF CLUB
You need a whole day to enjoy a game on the outlying island of Lantau (► 15). 18 holes.
✉ Valley Road, Discovery Bay, Lantau Island ☎ 2987 7271 🕐 Mon–Fri 8:30–3.15 ➧ Outlying Islands Pier, Central ⛳ Green fees HK$900

HONG KONG GOLF CLUB
This 36-hole course has practice putting greens, too. The famous golf club has three (more expensive) 18-hole courses at Fanling, New Territories (☎ 2670 1211), also open to visitors.
✉ 19 Island Road, Deepwater Bay, Hong Kong Island ☎ 2812 7070 🕐 May–Aug Mon–Fri 9:30–2.30. Sep–Apr Mon-Fri 9:30–1.30. Closed first Tue of every month 🚌 Bus 6 minibus from Central Bus Terminal ⛳ Green fees HK$600

NIGHTCLUBS

BIG APPLE

At weekends this place warms up around 2AM and keeps shaking until 6 in the morning.

✚ F8 ✉ 20 Luard Road, Wan Chai ☎ 2529 3461 🕙 Daily 9PM–6AM 🚇 Wan Chai

CATWALK

A glitzy entertainment complex with disco and karaoke rooms. 11 bands from around the world, resident Latin American salsa band, video wall. Free midweek; cover charge Thu, Fri and Sat.

✚ F7 ✉ New World Hotel, 22 Salisbury Road, Tsim Sha Tsui ☎ 2369 4111 ext 6380 🕙 Sun–Thu 9:30PM–3AM; Fri–Sat 9:30PM–4AM 🚇 Tsim Sha Tsui

JJs

This club has a pizza lounge, pool table and dartboard. The house band has been playing to enthusiastic packed audiences for some time. Happy hours 5:30PM–8:30PM. *Dim sum* hours 6PM–7:30PM.

✚ F8 🏨 Grand Hyatt Hotel, 1 Harbour Road, Wan Chai ☎ 2588 1234 🕙 Mon–Thu 5:30PM–2AM; Fri–Sat 5:30PM–3AM; Sun 9PM–2AM 🚇 Wan Chai

JOE BANANAS

Very trendy American-style bar, disco and restaurant. Long hours at weekends; men must wear a shirt with collar. Happy hours 11AM–9PM. Minimum age 21.

✚ F8 ✉ 23 Luard Road, Wan Chai ☎ 2529 1811 🕙 Daily Mon–Thu 11AM–5AM; Fri–Sat 11AM–6AM; Sun and holidays noon–4AM 🚇 Wan Chai

NEPTUNE DISCO 11

Live music and DJs entertain multiracial dancers. Cover charge varies with the season and day of the week, but in general this place offers the most dancing for the least expense.

✚ F8 ✉ 98–108 Jaffe Road, Wan Chai ☎ 2865 2238 🕙 Daily 9PM–7AM 🚇 Wan Chai

POST '97

Sultry Moroccan-style café, bar and club, open 24 hours over the weekend so the partying never stops.

✚ D8 ✉ UG/F Cosmos Building, 9–11 Lan Kwai Fong, Central ☎ 2810 9333 🕙 Mon–Thu 9AM–2AM; Sat 9AM–Sun 9AM 🚇 Central

ROY'S AT THE NEW CHINA MAX

A bar, disco and Pacific Rim restaurant. Pan-Asian decor with carved elephants and statuary, live bands and good DJs. No cover charge.

✚ G8 ✉ 11/F, Times Square, 1 Matheson Street, Causeway Bay ☎ 2506 2282 🕙 Tue, Fri, Sat 10:30PM–2AM 🚇 Causeway Bay

WEST WORLD

Chairman Mao – whose face finds its way into the décor – would hardly approve, but the pyjama-clad staff and busy dancers are hard at work in this small but trendy night-spot. The admission charge almost doubles at the weekend.

✚ F8 ✉ 4/F, New World Harbour View Hotel, 1 Harbour Road, Wan Chai ☎ 2824 1066 🕙 Daily 9:30PM–3AM 🚇 Wan Chai

Cover charges

It is always worth telephoning discos before you go to confirm the hours and cover charge. Many places have reduced rates during the week and/or include one or two drinks, but expect to pay HK$100+ on Fridays and Saturdays.

LIVE MUSIC

Nightlife on the island

Lan Kwai Fong, in Central, is where the trendy young *gweilos* (➤ 9, panel) hang out. The streets are often as lively, and as crowded, as the bars, bistros and clubs. Wan Chai, once very seedy, is now much more attractive, with lots of cheaper Western and Chinese restaurants; North Point, in the east of the island, is beginning to develop a nightlife of its own. Stanley, too, has a unique atmosphere – more relaxed and meditative than other areas.

CARNEGIE'S

An interesting nightspot where the music shifts genre regularly. Cover charge only for men at weekends. Local bands, lovely atmosphere. Visit only if you enjoy loud music and a crush on the dance floor.

➕ F8 ✉ 53 Lockhart Road, Wan Chai ☎ 2866 6289
🕐 Thu 7PM–10PM; Sat 7PM–midnight; Sun 7PM–11PM
🚇 Wan Chai

DELANEY'S, TSIM SHA TSUI

The design recreates a Victorian Irish general store-cum-pub, and there's live traditional music and Irish food – even Guinness. In the branch in Luard Road, Wan Chai, there is also a Sunday evening jam session.

➕ F6 ✉ G/F, Multifield Plaza, 3–7a Prat Avenue, Tsim Sha Tsui ☎ 2301 3980
🕐 Mon–Thu noon–3AM; Fri–Sat noon–5AM; Sun noon–2AM
🚇 Tsim Sha Tsui

HARDY'S FOLK CLUB

Not as folksy as its name suggests but an alternative to the heavy metal, rock or jazz venues for those with a taste for folk. Go there just to listen and have a drink, or perhaps make a night of it with a meal.

➕ D8 ✉ 35 D'Aguilar Street, Central ☎ 2522 4448
🕐 Daily 5:30PM–2AM
🚇 Central

THE JAZZ CLUB

Too many places in Hong Kong are squashed into anonymous buildings, but the cramped confines here are just what is required. The Jazz Club, one of the few places that can be relied on for quality jazz, regularly features musicians from all over the world, drinks are reasonably priced and cover charges, high for international big names, are dropped for local acts. Seats can be reserved but must be claimed before 9PM at weekends. The alternative atmosphere and the lively audience make for a great night out.

➕ D8 ✉ 2/F, California Building, 34–6 D'Aguilar Street, Central ☎ 2845 8477
🕐 Daily 9:30PM–2AM
🚇 Central

NED KELLY'S LAST STAND

The best place in Hong Kong for traditional and Dixieland honking jazz, belted out by a resident band, with convivial atmosphere, pub food and no cover charge.

➕ F6 ✉ 11a Ashley Road, Tsim Sha Tsui ☎ 2376 0562
🕐 Daily 9PM–2AM 🚇 Tsim Sha Tsui

THE WANCH

A sociable and deservedly popular place, originally a folk club. Its live music now includes rock. No cover charge, reasonably priced drinks and usually very good music indeed. Can get very crowded, so arrive early.

➕ F8 ✉ 54 Jaffe Road, Wan Chai ☎ 2861 1621 🕐 Daily 9PM–2AM 🚇 Wan Chai

PUBS

ACROPOLIS
There's no music at this dedicated watering hole but a sociable set of customers who often fill the place to capacity.
🔲 D8 ✉ G/F, Corner 11 Tower, 21 D'Aguilar Street, Central ☎ 2877 3668
🕐 Daily 11AM–3AM 🚇 Central

BERLIN
Five-hour happy hour reigns every night, with disco and a karaoke room. After 10PM it is a straightforward disco.
🔲 D8 ✉ 19 Lan Kwai Fong, Central ☎ 2530 3093
🕐 Daily 5PM–10PM 🚇 Central

BULL & BEAR
Very popular with expatriate office workers during the happy hour (5–8 weeknights). No live music. British-style setting with oak beams, and English bar food.
🔲 E8 ✉ G/F, Hutchinson House, 10 Harcourt Road, Central
☎ 2525 7436 🕐 Mon–Sat 8AM–2AM; Sun noon–midnight
🚇 Admiralty

DICKENS BAR
A Dickensian place – one of Hong Kong's best and most deservedly fashionable bars. Bands change constantly – Irish, West Indian, Indonesian and Filipino – and there's a Sunday afternoon trumpet-blasting jazz session.
🔲 G8 ✉ LG/F, Excelsior Hotel, 281 Gloucester Road, Causeway Bay ☎ 2894 8888
🕐 Mon–Sat noon–1:30AM; Sun 3PM–midnight 🚇 Causeway Bay

MAD DOGS, CENTRAL
Another pub with a gregarious crowd.

Regular live music, individual singers or a band get going after the 4–8 happy hour. Another happy hour between 10 and 11.
🔲 D8 ✉ Basement, Capital Building, 1 D'Aguilar Street, Central ☎ 2810 1000
🕐 Mon–Fri, Sun 8AM–1:30AM; Sat 10AM–3AM

MAD DOGS, KOWLOON
A sister bar to the one in Central, but with a larger quota of tourists and a more cosmopolitan atmosphere. Live music Tuesday, Thursday, Sunday; happy hour 4–8 every evening.
🔲 F6 ✉ 32 Nathan Road, Tsim Sha Tsui ☎ 2301 2222
🕐 Mon–Thu, Sun 8AM–2AM; Fri–Sat 8AM–4AM 🚇 Tsim Sha Tsui

OSCAR'S
Very trendy, fan-cooled bar opening on to the street where amiable crowds gather. Few places to sit down. The food is good in the separate restaurant, but the main activity is drinking and chatting.
🔲 D8 ✉ G/F and basement, 2 Lan Kwai Fong, Central
☎ 2861 3777 🕐 Mon–Sat 11–2; Sun 11–12 🚇 Central

SCHNURRBART
A German bier-keller and restaurant serving heady German draughts and some 25 types of schnapps. A juke-box plays Western pop hits.
🔲 D8 ✉ 29 D'Aguilar Street, Central ☎ 2523 4700
🕐 Mon–Thu noon–12:30AM; Fri–Sat noon–1:30AM; Sun 6PM–12:30AM 🚇 Central

Nightlife in Kowloon
Because of its budget accommodation, Kowloon has lots of inexpensive, casual bars, many with an Australian flavour, such as the Kangaroo, overlooking Kowloon Park, or Ned Kelly's. In addition there are the many 'hostess' bars, where a drink and a girl to talk to come in a package. Some of these, including Bottoms Up, in Hankow Road, are almost a national institution.

LUXURY HOTELS

Prices

Expect to pay for a double room
per night

Luxury
over HK$1,000

Mid-Range
HK$700–HK$1,000

Budget
under HK$700

Also ➤ 85, panel.

HONG KONG ISLAND

CHARTERHOUSE
A pleasant little hotel tucked away in Wan Chai. Lots of facilities, near major shopping areas. Compact but very comfortable rooms.
✚ G8 ✉ 209–19 Wan Chai Road, Wan Chai ☎ 2833 5566; fax 2833 5888; internet www.charterhouse.com
🚇 Causeway Bay or Wan Chai

CONRAD
Rooms are spacious and individually designed with every comfort. Some of the best views in Hong Kong are from the amazing top floors. Fitness centre, pool, and beautiful interiors.
✚ E8 ✉ Pacific Place, 88 Queensway ☎ 2521 3838; fax 2521 3888; internet www.conrad.com.hk
🚇 Admiralty

THE EXCELSIOR
Pleasant and casual with nice rooms and an enormous range of facilities, right up to the two covered tennis courts on the roof. Convenient for shopping and nightlife.
✚ G8 ✉ 281 Gloucester Road, Causeway Bay ☎ 2894 8888; fax 2895 6459; e-mail mandarin-oriental.com/...
🚇 Causeway Bay

J W MARRIOTT
A pleasant and peaceful place to stay in the heart of Central, near major tourist attractions and with plenty of facilities. Spacious, sunny rooms, all with two floor-to-ceiling

glass walls. Outdoor pool, fitness centre.
✚ E8 ✉ Pacific Place, 88 Queensway ☎ 2810 8366; fax 2845 0737; internet www.conrad.com.hk
🚇 Admiralty

MANDARIN ORIENTAL
The very central Mandarin Oriental has a long tradition of impeccable service. Well-appointed rooms, with superb attention to detail. Helpful staff, classy shopping centre, great pool, excellent restaurants.
✚ E8 ✉ 5 Connaught Road, Central ☎ 2522 0111; fax 2810 6190; e-mail mandarin-oriental.com/...
🚇 Central

NEW WORLD HARBOUR VIEW
A very modern, bright hotel with massive glass walls and a prime location: the high floors have harbour views. Pleasantly appointed, spacious rooms. Enormous fitness centre and swimming pool. There is even a rooftop jogging track.
✚ F8 ✉ 1 Harbour Road, Wan Chai ☎ 2802 8888; fax 2802 8833 🚇 Wan Chai

KOWLOON

THE PENINSULA
A landmark, cultural icon, tourist attraction in its own right, and the last word in style. Very popular afternoon tea.
✚ F6 ✉ Salisbury Road, Tsim Sha Tsui ☎ 2366 6251; fax 2722 4170; internet www.peninsula.com/phk.htm
🚇 Tsim Sha Tsui

MID-RANGE HOTELS

HONG KONG ISLAND

EMERALD
Comfortable rooms, harbour views and easy access to the rest of Hong Kong Island.
➕ C7 ✉ 152 Connaught Road West, Sheung Wan ☎ 2546 8111; fax 2559 0255 🚇 Sheung Wan

HARBOUR VIEW INTERNATIONAL HOUSE
Over 12 free shuttle buses a day to Causeway Bay and the Star Ferry. Try to obtain a room with a harbour view.
➕ F8 ✉ 4 Harbour Road, Wan Chai ☎ 2801 0111; fax 2802 9063 🚇 Wan Chai

NEW CATHAY
Nudging into the expensive category but lacking many facilities. Single rooms are the best value because, unusually among Hong Kong hotels, they cost considerably less than doubles.
➕ H8 ✉ 17 Tung Lo Wan Road, Causeway Bay ☎ 2577 8211; fax 2576 9365 🚇 Causeway Bay

NEW HARBOUR
Only minutes from the MTR station and bus and tram routes to the east and west.
➕ F8 ✉ 41–9 Hennessy Road, Wan Chai ☎ 2861 1166; fax 2865 6111 🚇 Wan Chai

THE WESLEY
Close to train, tram and bus routes, with a café and decent international restaurant.
➕ F8 ✉ 22 Hennessy Road, Wan Chai ☎ 2866 6688; fax 2866 6633 🚇 Wan Chai

KOWLOON

EATON
Large with lots of facilities, including restaurants and a bar (but no pool or sports amenities), and a range of room rates. A short hop on any bus stopping outside the front door takes you to Tsim Sha Tsui.
➕ F5 ✉ 380 Nathan Road, Yau Ma Tei ☎ 2782 1818; fax 2782 5563 🚇 Jordan

IMPERIAL
No restaurants or nightlife in-house, but you don't need them at this end of Nathan Road. Just over 200 rooms.
➕ F6 ✉ 30–4 Nathan Road, Tsim Sha Tsui ☎ 2366 2201; fax 2311 2360 e-mail reservation@imperialhotel.com.hk 🚇 Tsim Sha Tsui

INTERNATIONAL
Right in the heart of Tsim Sha Tsui. Reasonable restaurants and rooms with balconies that afford neon views.
➕ F6 ✉ 33 Cameron Road, Tsim Sha Tsui ☎ 2366 3381; fax 2369 5381 🚇 Tsim Sha Tsui

SHAMROCK
A good-value no-frills hotel with an economically priced restaurant. Buses are on the doorstep and the MTR is only steps away.
➕ F5 ✉ 223 Nathan Road, Yau Ma Tei ☎ 2735 2271; fax 2736 354; e-mail shamrock@iohk.com 🚇 Jordan

Hotel tips
A travel agent should be able to obtain sizeable discounts on the room rates in the luxury and mid-range hotels. Try to get a breakfast buffet included because it is often a substantial repast.

Above average youth hostel
The 366-room YMCA, also called the Salisbury (✉ 41 Salisbury Road, Tsim Sha Tsui ☎ 2369 2211; fax 2739 9315) has a lot going for it: mid-range room rates, a location that's ideal for shopping and convenient to the Star Ferry, plus an inexpensive self-service restaurant, free use of swimming pool and lots of other facilities normally associated with top-class establishments.

BUDGET ACCOMMODATION

Chungking Mansions

Chungking Mansions, a vast, crumbling and dingy shopping/housing block in Nathan Road, has such an image problem – it used to be raided regularly by the police for illegal immigrants – that the budget accommodation there has never quite been able to recover. Now, however, fire regulations have been enforced and unlicensed premises closed down. The lifts remain claustrophobic and the stairways are even worse, but this is still the place for budget rooms – (and budget Indian restaurants ➤ 66).

HONG KONG ISLAND

GARDEN VIEW INTERNATIONAL HOUSE (YWCA)
The only budget hotel-style accommodation on Hong Kong Island that has an outdoor swimming pool (closed in winter). Book well in advance.
➕ D9 ✉ 1 MacDonnell Road, Central ☎ 2877 3737; fax 2845 6263 🚇 Bus 12A from Central Bus Terminal or minibus from outside City Hall

NOBLE HOSTEL
A reliable establishment offering rooms with both shared and private bath. A double with private bathroom at HK$350 is a gem of a bargain on Hong Kong Island.
➕ G8 ✉ Flat A3, 17/F, 27 Paterson Street, Causeway Bay ☎ 2576 6148; fax 2577 0847 🚇 Causeway Bay

KOWLOON

BOOTH LODGE
Named after the founder of the Salvation Army (which operates the hotel). Well-run, with clean rooms, efficient service and a small café.
➕ F5 ✉ 11 Wing Sing Lane, Yau Ma Tei ☎ 2771 9266; fax 2385 1140 🚇 Yau Ma Tei

CARITAS BLANCHI LODGE
Tidy, clean and friendly. Facilities, though limited, include a laundry and restaurants.
➕ F5 ✉ 4 Cliff Road, Yau Ma Tei ☎ 2388 1111; fax 2770 6669 🚇 Yau Ma Tei

CARITAS LODGE (BOUNDARY STREET)
Basic and roomy with a coffee shop, laundry facilities and some triple rooms.
➕ G3 ✉ 134 Boundary Street, Kowlooni ☎ 2339 3777; fax 2338 2864 🚇 Prince Edward, then bus 2D

CHUNGKING HOUSE
The best place to stay in any of the blocks of Chungking Mansions. Rooms are basic but they are smart and well-managed. Restaurant and laundry facilities.
➕ F6 ✉ Block A, 4–5/F, Chungking Mansion, 40 Nathan Road, Tsim Sha Tsui ☎ 2366 5362; fax 2721 3570 🚇 Tsim Sha Tsui

KING'S HOTEL
Reasonably priced and pleasant rooms, and well suited for a walk into Tsim Sha Tsui. Close to MTR. Restaurant serves Western, Chinese and Thai food. Coffee shop, laundry service.
➕ F4 ✉ 473–473A Nathan Road, Yau Ma Tei ☎ 2780 1281; fax 2782 1833 🚇 Yau Ma Tei

YMCA INTERNATIONAL HOUSE
Nearly 300 rooms in a modern block with basic amenities at competitive rates. No membership required.
➕ F4 ✉ 23 Waterloo Road, Yau Ma Tei ☎ 2771 9111; fax 2388 5926 🚇 Yau Ma Tei

HONG KONG
travel facts

ARRIVING & DEPARTING

Before you go

- All visitors must hold a valid passport, and the length of a visa-free visit depends on citizenship: one month for American, German and Greek citizens; three months for Commonwealth and most European citizens; six months for British citizens.
- All other citizens should consult the Chinese Embassy in their country or write to: ✉ Immigration Department, 7 Gloucester Road, Wan Chai, Hong Kong ☎ 852 2829 3000
- No vaccinations are required.

When to go

- The ideal time is between October and mid-December – days are warm and fresh, nights cool and comfortable.
- If you have a choice, avoid June–September, when the weather is uncomfortable and there is a risk of typhoons.

Climate

- Spring and autumn are usually warm, but spring is more unsettled, with rain common.
- Winters are usually comfortable, although there are occasional cold spells when a jacket of some kind is essential and you may need a light coat.
- Summer is very hot and humid, with nearly 400mm (16in) of rain on average each month. The clammy heat sometimes gives way to violent typhoons.

Typhoons

- Called hurricanes in the Atlantic, typhoons (from *dai foo*, the Chinese for 'big wind') hit Hong Kong between July and September. There is a well-rehearsed procedure for dealing with these storms and hotels post up the appropriate storm signal:
- Storm Signal 1: Typhoon within 800km of Hong Kong.
- Storm Signal 3: Typhoon on its way; be prepared.
- Storm Signal 8: Stay in your hotel; dangerous, gusty winds.

Arriving

- All flights land at Chek Lap Kok, the new international airport, which is 23 minutes by rail from Central, 18 minutes from Kowloon.
- Take the shuttle to the Airport Express railway station or to the taxi rank.
- There are public buses, hotel buses, and a hotel shuttle bus service, as well as taxis and the train, but the train is the most efficient way of getting to town.

Customs regulations

- The duty-free allowance is 1 litre of spirits and 200 cigarettes.
- Export and import licences are required for any amount of ivory taken out of the country.

Departure tax

- Anyone over 12 years old pays HK$100. Payment in Hong Kong dollars only.

ESSENTIAL FACTS

Tourist information

- HKTA (Hong Kong Tourist Association) has two offices:
  ✉ Star Ferry Concourse, Tsim Sha Tsui
  🕐 Mon–Fri 8–6; Sat, Sun, public holidays 9–5
  ✉ Shop 8, Basement, Jardine House, Connaught Place, Central 🕐 Mon–Fri 9–6; Sat 9–1
- For telephone information:

☎ 2807 6177 Mon–Fri 8–6; Sat, Sun, public holidays 9–5

Travel insurance
- Take out a health and accident policy – you will have to pay for medication or hospitalisation.

Opening hours
- Offices: Mon–Fri 9–5; Sat 9–1
- Banks: Mon–Fri 9–4:30; Sat 9–12:30
- Post offices: Mon–Fri 8–6; Sat 8–2
- Shops: Mon–Sun 10–6, often 10–9 in tourist areas.

National holidays
- Dates of the Chinese lunar festivals vary from year to year.
- New Year's Day (1 Jan)
- Chinese New Year (1999: 16–18 Feb; 2000: 4–6 Feb)
- Good Friday and Easter Monday (1999: 2 and 5 Apr; 2000: 21 and 24 Apr)
- Ching Ming Festival (1999: 5 Apr; 2000: 6 Jun)
- Dragon Boat Festival (1999: 18 Jun; 2000: 6 Jun)
- Sino-Japanese War Victory Day (1999: 16 Aug; 2000: 21 Aug)
- Mid-Autumn Festival (1999: 24 Sep; 2000: 12 Sep)
- Cheung Yeung Festival (1999: 17 Oct; 2000 21 Aug)
- Christmas Day and Boxing Day (25 and 26 Dec)

Money matters
- Traveller's cheques can often be used as payment or cashed at banks or moneychangers. Always check the exchange rate before making any transaction; banks offer the best rates.
- Credit cards – Visa, Access (MasterCard), American Express and Diners Club – are widely accepted for purchases in shops and restaurants. In small shops make sure (illegal) commission is not being added.
- Credit cards can be used to obtain cash from banks and ATM machines. Some Hong Kong Bank teller machines provide 24-hour HK$ withdrawal facilities for Visa and MasterCard holders. Amex holders have the same facility at some Jetco ATMs, as well as the Express ATMs.

Etiquette
- Rules of etiquette are similar to those in Europe or North America, but Hong Kong is a fast city so don't be surprised when people jump queues or fail to queue at all.
- Shaking hands with either sex is common practice and the exchanging of business cards, presented with both hands, is even more common.
- Chinese names begin with the family name, so Mr Tan Wing Chan, for example: is Mr Tan; the adoption of a Western first name is very common.
- A service charge is usually added to restaurant bills, but an extra 10 per cent is often still expected. Round up taxi fares to the next dollar or two.

Lone travellers
- For lone travellers Hong Kong is similar to, and often safer than, most European or North American cities; take commonsense precautions.
- Public transport at night is as safe as it is during the day.

Student travellers
- There are few discounts for ISIC (International Student Identity Card) holders.

- The Student Travel Bureau ✉ Room 1021, 10/F, Star House, Tsim Sha Tsui ☎ 2730 3269 dispenses a free booklet detailing retail outlets with student discounts.
- Some places of interest have a reduced admission charge for students.

Places of worship

- Protestant Evangelical Community Church ✉ 4th floor YMCA, Salisbury Road, Tsim Sha Tsui ☎ 2789 0071
- The Roman Catholic Cathedral ✉ 16 Cairn Road, Mid Levels, Hong Kong Island ☎ 2522 8212
- Jewish Ohel Leah Synagogue ✉ 70 Robinson Road, Central
- Kowloon Mosque ✉ Kowloon Park ☎ 2724 0095

Time differences

- Hong Kong is 8 hours ahead of GMT.

Toilets

- Most toilets are Western in style.
- Hotels and shopping centres are the best places to find clean toilets.
- In older places, the MTR and KCR, toilets are often of the squat type common in Asia.

Electricity

- The current is 200/220 volts, 50 cycles alternating current (AC).
- Most wall outlets take three square pins; some older ones take three large round pins.
- US appliances require a voltage converter and a plug adaptor.

PUBLIC TRANSPORT

Trains

- The MTR is the quickest way to hop between shopping areas, and between Hong Kong Island and Tsim Sha Tsui; for access to the New Territories use the interchange station at Kowloon Tong and change to the KCR (Kowloon–Canton Railway), which travels north to the border at Lo Wu.
- Stations are located by a symbol and there are clear instructions for operating machines.
- Machines issue thin plastic tickets; insert the exact change (available at machines or at information/ticket counters).
- Fares are between HK$4 and HK$12.50. Enquiries ☎ 2750 0170

Trams

- Trams run only on Hong Kong Island's north side, but there is a useful route between Kennedy Town in the west and Causeway Bay in the east.
- Destinations are marked on the front in English.
- The fixed fare of HK$1.60 (80¢ children) is dropped in the paybox when leaving the tram.

Buses

- Travelling by bus is not recommended (except for trips to the south side of Hong Kong Island); the MTR is faster and easier to use.
- The fixed fare is marked on the bus as you enter and pay; no change is given.
- Minibuses (red and yellow) carrying 14–16 passengers can be flagged down almost anywhere along their routes.
- Maxicabs (green and yellow) also carry 14–16 passengers but stop only at designated places.
- For a short stay it is not worth mastering minibuses or maxicabs; posted destinations are often illegible, and fares on

minibuses vary with the length of journey.

Where to get maps

- MTR maps are available at the airport and most hotel lobbies.
- MTR stations dispense a free guide to the system.
- Tourist Association (HKTA) offices (▶ 88–9) have a free map showing bus routes and fares.

Discounts

- For the MTR, KCR, buses, some ferries, and several other forms of public transport, you can buy an Octopus ticket. It costs HK$150, for which you get a little over HK$100 worth of travel. The other HK$50 is refundable when you leave. You can buy the card, and recharge it as often as you want, at any ticket office. It will save you finding change for bus journeys and queueing up for tickets in the busy MTR. Check your ticket balance at any railway station or look at the machine as you go through the barrier.
- Further discounts for students, OAPs and children.

Taxis

- The flagfare is HK$14.50 and after 2km the fare increases by HK$1.30 for every 200m. There is a HK$5 call-out charge if a taxi is booked by phone and comes to your pick-up point.
- Using one of the tunnels between Hong Kong Island and Kowloon costs from HK$20 to HK$45, depending on which tunnel is used.
- A 'For Hire' sign is displayed in the windscreen; at night a 'Taxi' sign is lit up on the roof.
- Taxis cannot stop at bus stops or on a yellow line.
- Taxis are good value, but most drivers don't speak much English.

MEDIA & COMMUNICATIONS

Telephones

- Local calls are free for subscribers, but public phones charge HK$1 per call and sometimes only take HK$2 coins without giving change. Pressing the 'FC' (follow-on call) button before hanging up allows a second call.
- It is easier to use a Phonecard (HK$50, HK$100 and HK$250), especially for an IDD (International Direct Dialling) call. 7–Eleven stores and many shops sell phonecards.
- Some telephone boxes accept only phonecards or only coins; others accept either.
- For IDD calls, dial 001, followed by the country code and then the area code (minus any initial 0) and number. Dial 013 for information about international calls.

Post offices

- On Hong Kong Island the General Post Office is next to the Star Ferry Concourse in Central.
- In Kowloon the main post office is at 10 Middle Road, off the lower end of Nathan Road.
- Letters and postcards to destinations outside South-East Asia cost HK$3.20 for the first 10g, plus HK$1.30 for each additional gram.
- The Speedpost service will cut the usual five-day service to Europe or North America by about half.

Newspapers

- There are two English-language daily newspapers: *South China Morning Post* and *Hong Kong Standard*. The *SCMP* has the better coverage for international and local news.
- International papers with Asian editions are the *Asian Wall Street Journal*, *USA Today* and the *International Herald Tribune*.

Magazines

- *Time*, *Newsweek*, *The Economist* and the regional *Asiaweek* are widely available.
- The *Far East Economic Review* is best for business and news.
- For entertainment listings look for the free, bi-weekly *Hong Kong Magazine* or the Hong Kong Tourist Association's free, weekly – *Hong Kong This Week* and *Hong Kong Diary*.

International newsagents

- International newspapers and magazines are available in bookshops and hotel kiosks.
- The pavement newsagent outside the Star Ferry terminal in Tsim Sha Tsui and the bookshop next to the ferry terminal in Central have a good selection.

Radio

- English-language stations include the BBC World Service: see daily English-language newspapers for details.

Television

- There are two English-language stations (TVB Pearl and ATV World) and two Cantonese-language stations.
- Many hotels subscribe to Star TV satellite television.

EMERGENCIES

Sensible precautions

- Hong Kong is very crowded, night and day, and professional pickpockets and thieves are able to capitalise on this.
- Keep wallets and purses secure.
- Keep traveller's cheques separate from the invoice that lists their numbers.
- Don't leave valuables where you can't see them at all times.
- Keep travel documents and money in a hotel safe.

Lost property

- ✉ Admiralty MTR station
  🕐 Mon–Sat 8–7 ☎ 2861 0020

Medical treatment

- Outpatient departments of public or private hospitals provide emergency treatment.
- Private doctors (see 'Physicians and Surgeons' in the Yellow Pages) charge HK$150 per visit on average. This usually includes three days' medication.
- Public hospitals: Queen Mary Hospital ✉ Pok Fu Lam Road, Hong Kong Island ☎ 2819 2111. Queen Elizabeth Hospital ✉ Wylie Road, Yau Ma Tei, Kowloon ☎ 2710 2111. Kwong Wah Hospital ✉ 25 Waterloo Road, Yau Ma Tei, Kowloon ☎ 2332 2311
- Private hospitals: Hong Kong Central ✉ 1B Lower Albert Road, Central, Hong Kong Island ☎ 2849 6301. Adventist ✉ 40 Stubbs Road, Wan Chai, Hong Kong Island ☎ 2574 6211 Baptist ✉ 222 Waterloo Road, Kowloon Tong ☎ 2337 4141

Medicines

- Watson's and Manning's are the biggest chain stores dispensing medicines (listed under 'Chemists' in the Yellow Pages) and are usually open until 8PM.

- A full range of pharmaceuticals is readily available, but bring special medicines with you.

Emergency phone numbers

- Police   )
- Fire   ) ☎ 999
- Ambulance)

Embassies and consulates

- Australia ✉ 23rd and 24th Floors, Harbour Centre, 25 Harbour Road, Wan Chai ☎ 2827 8881
- Canada ✉ 11th–14th Floors, Tower One, Exchange Square, 8 Connaught Place, Central ☎ 2810 4321
- Germany ✉ 21st Floor, United Centre, 95 Queensway, Central ☎ 2529 8855
- UK ✉ c/o Overseas Visa Section, Immigration Department, 2nd Floor, Wan Chai Tower Two, 7 Gloucester Road, Wan Chai ☎ 2824 6111
- USA ✉ 26 Garden Road, Central ☎ 2523 9011

LANGUAGE

- Hong Kong has two official languages: English and Chinese. English is spoken widely in business circles and in tourist areas, but not every Chinese person understands English as many have come to live here from mainland China. To avoid confusion and frustration, get the hotel receptionist to write down your destination in Chinese.
- The Cantonese dialect is spoken in Hong Kong.
- You may come across some unfamiliar English words in Hong Kong: *amah*, housekeeper or servant; *chop*, a personal seal used in business; *dai pai dong*, street food stall; *shroff*, cashier, often at car parks; *godown*, warehouse; *wetmarket*, a fresh food market; *congee*, a savoury porridge made from rice.
- A few words of Cantonese go a long way in establishing rapport – and in places off the beaten track may prove useful.

Can you speak English? neih wuih mwuih gong ying mahn?
good morning jóu sahn
how are you? néih hou ma?
hello (only on the phone) wai!
thank you (for a favour) mgòi
thank you (for a gift) dò jeh
please mgòi
excuse me mgòi
I'm sorry deui mjyuh
yes haih *or* hou
no mhaih *or* mhou
where? bin douh?
how many/how much? géi dõ?
how much is it? géi dõ chin?
airport fèi gèi chèung
bus bā si
tram dihn chè
taxi dik sí
what time is it? géi dim jung?
three o'clock sáam dim jung
tea chàh
sugar tòhng
beer bè jáu
dollar mān
US dollar méih gàm
Hong Kong Hèung Góng
Kowloon Gáu Lùhng
The New Territories Sàn Gaai
Peak Tram Laahm Chè
The Peak Sàn Déng

0	leng	20	yih sahp
1	yāt	21	yih sahp yat
2	yih	30	sàam sahp
3	sàam	31	sàam sahp yat
4	sei	40	sei sahp
5	ngh	50	ngh sah
6	luhk	60	luhk sahp
7	chát	70	chát sahp
8	baat	80	baat sahp
9	gáu	90	gáu sahp
10	sahp	100	yāt baak
11	sahp yāt	1,000	yāt chihn

INDEX

CityPack
Hong Kong

Written by   Sean Sheehan and Pat Levy
Edited, designed and produced by
   AA Publishing
Maps   © The Automobile Association 1996,1999
Fold-out map   © RV Reise- und Verkehrsverlag Munich · Stuttgart
   © Cartography: GeoData

Distributed in the United Kingdom by AA Publishing, Norfolk House, Priestley Road, Basingstoke, Hampshire, RG24 9NY.

© The Automobile Association 1996, 1999
First published   1996
Revised second edition   1999

ISBN 0 7495 1896 0

Published by AA Publishing (a trading name of Automobile Association Developments Limited, whose registered office is Norfolk House, Priestley Road, Basingstoke, Hampshire RG24 9NY. Registered number 1878835).

Origination by BTB Colour Reproduction Ltd, Whitchurch, Hampshire
Printed and bound by Dai Nippon Printing Co (Hong Kong) Ltd.

Acknowledgements
The Automobile Association wishes to thank the following photographers, libraries and associations for their assistance in the preparation of this book
MUSEUM OF HISTORY, Hong Kong 39a, 39b. REX FEATURES LTD 12. SPECTRUM COLOUR LIBRARY 5b, 21a, 49b, 87b. MUSEUM & ART GALLERY, UNIVERSITY OF HONG KONG 26. TRAVEL INK/DEREK ALLAN 24
The remaining pictures are held in the Association's own library (AA PHOTO LIBRARY) and were taken by ALEX KOUPRIANOFF with the exception of pages 13a and 20, which were taken by INGRID MOREJOHN.

Cover photographs
Main picture: James Davis Travel Photography.
Insets: AA Photo Library (Alex Kouprianoff)

ORIGINAL COPY EDITOR *Lynn Bresler*
INDEXER *Marie Lorimer*
REVISION VERIFIERS *Sean Sheehan and Pat Levy*
SECOND EDITION UPDATED BY *OutHouse Publishing Services*

Titles in the CityPack series
● Amsterdam ● Atlanta ● Bangkok ● Barcelona ● Beijing ● Berlin ● Boston ●
● Brussels & Bruges ● Chicago ● Dublin ● Florence ● Hong Kong ● Istanbul ●
● Lisbon ● London ● Los Angeles ● Madrid ● Miami ● Montréal ● Moscow ●
● Munich ● New York ● Paris ● Prague ● Rome ● San Francisco ●Seattle ●
● Shanghai ● Singapore ● Sydney ● Tokyo ● Toronto ● Venice ● Vienna ●
● Washington DC ●